BALLOON

COLORING BOOK

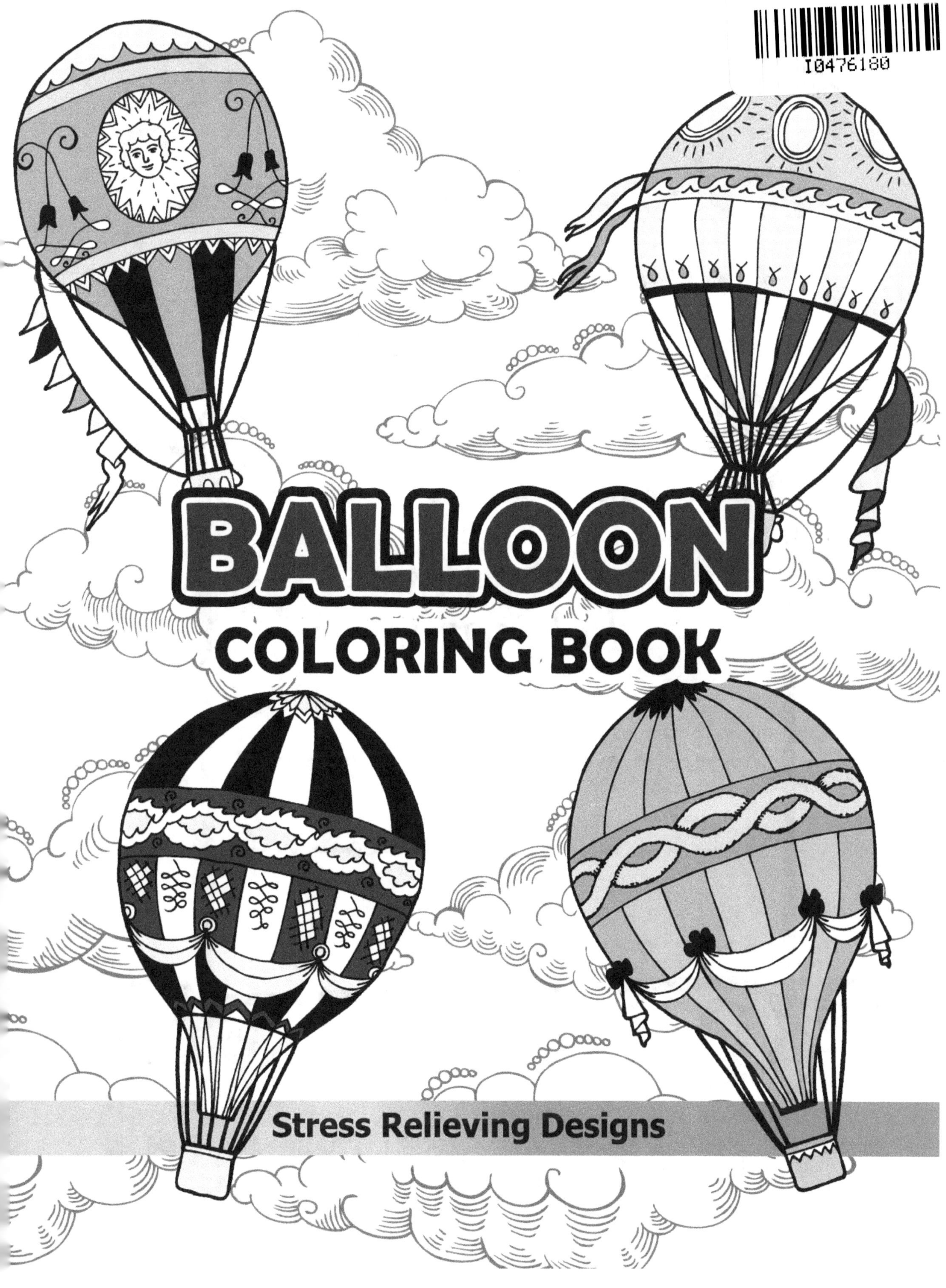

Stress Relieving Designs

COLORING BOOKS FOR ADULTS

This Book

belongs to

TEST YOUR COLOR

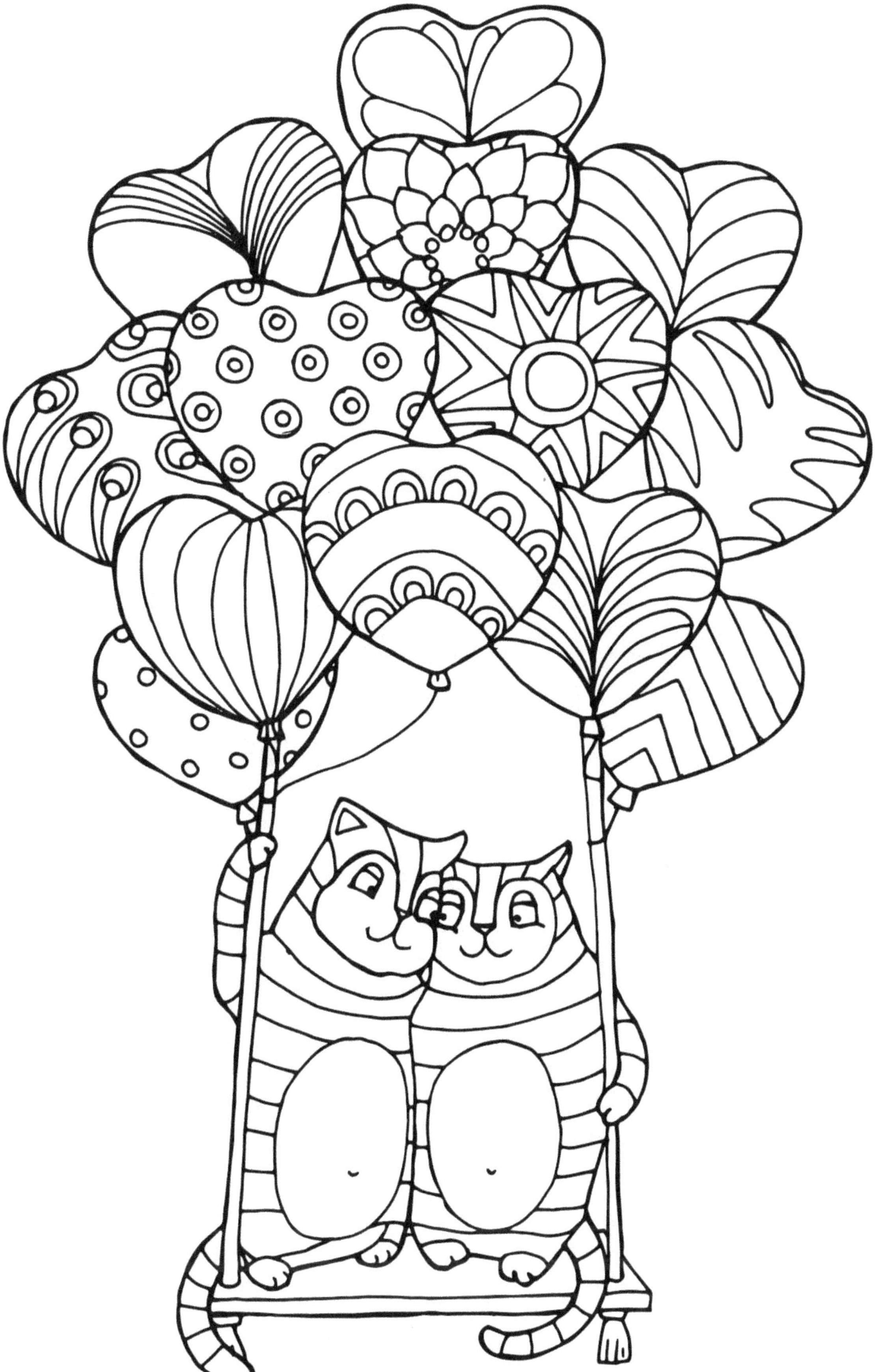

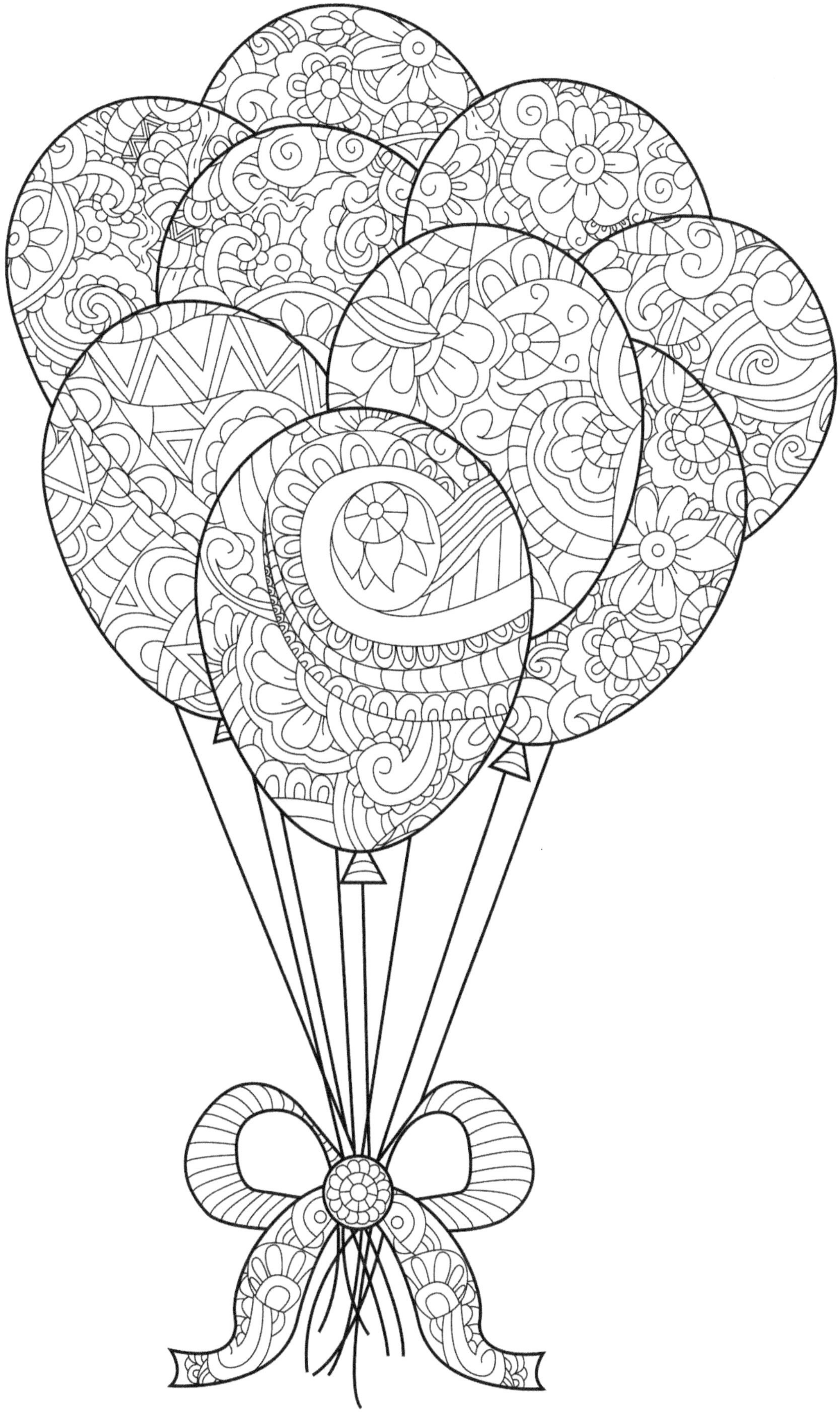

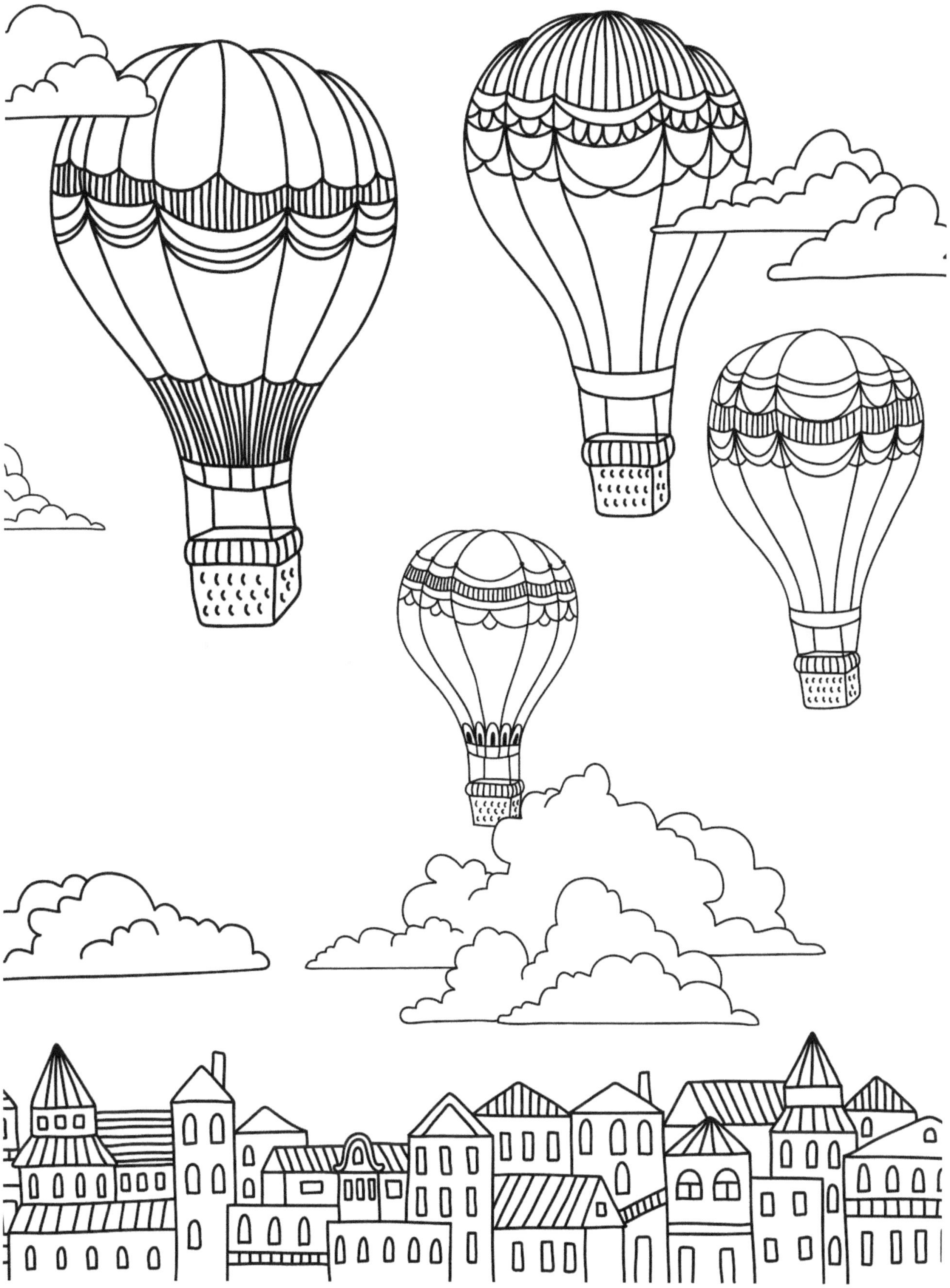

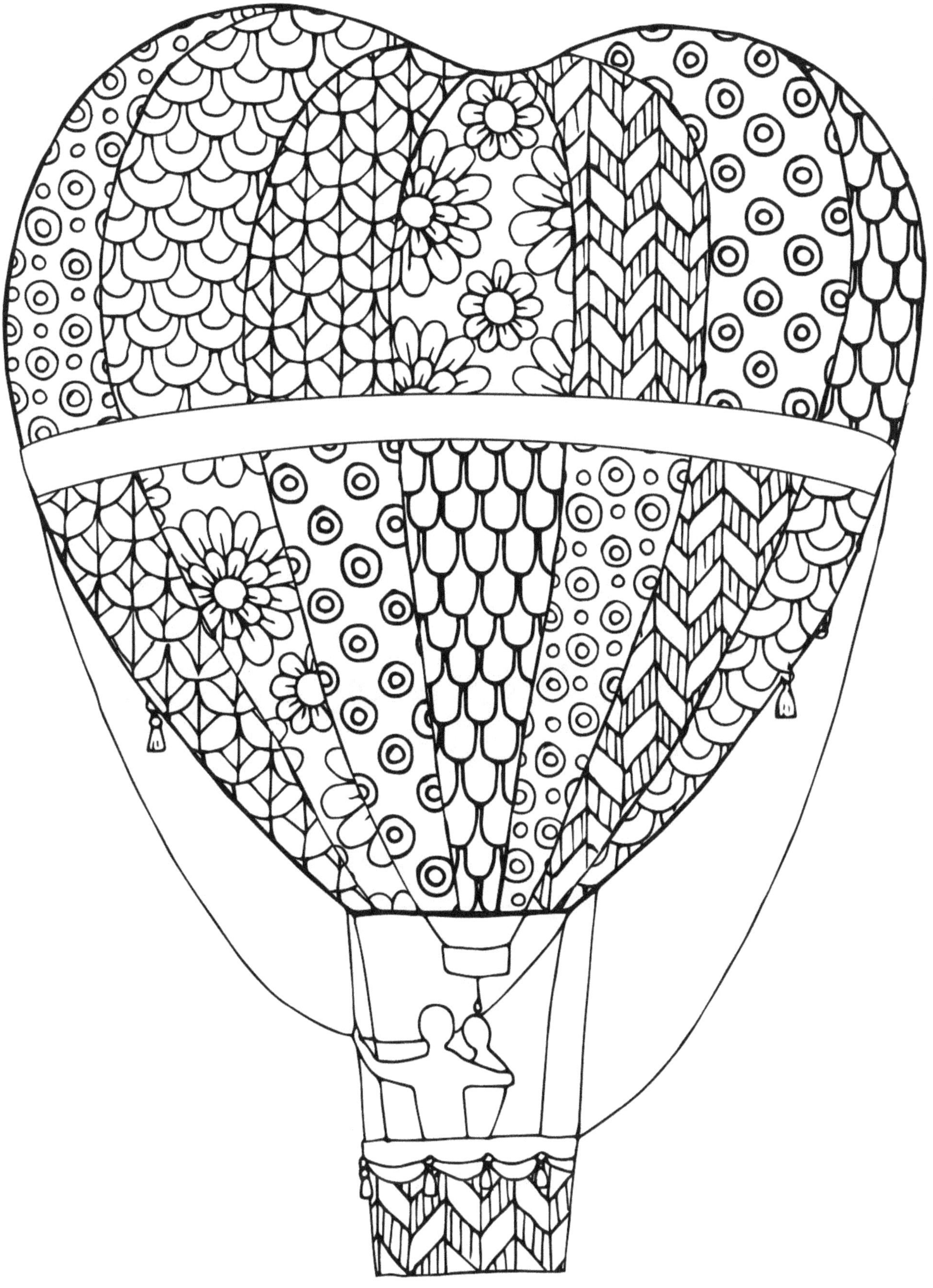

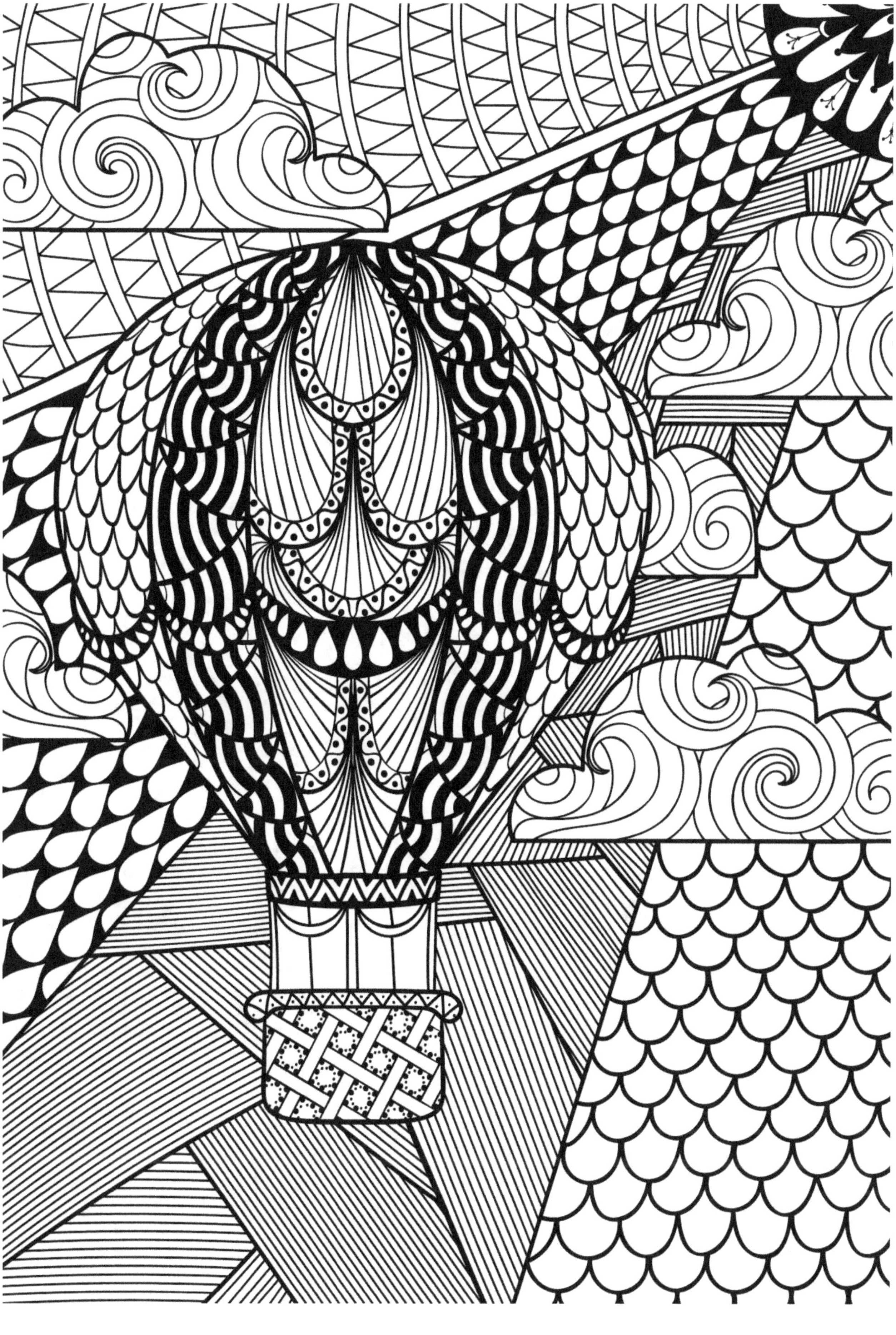

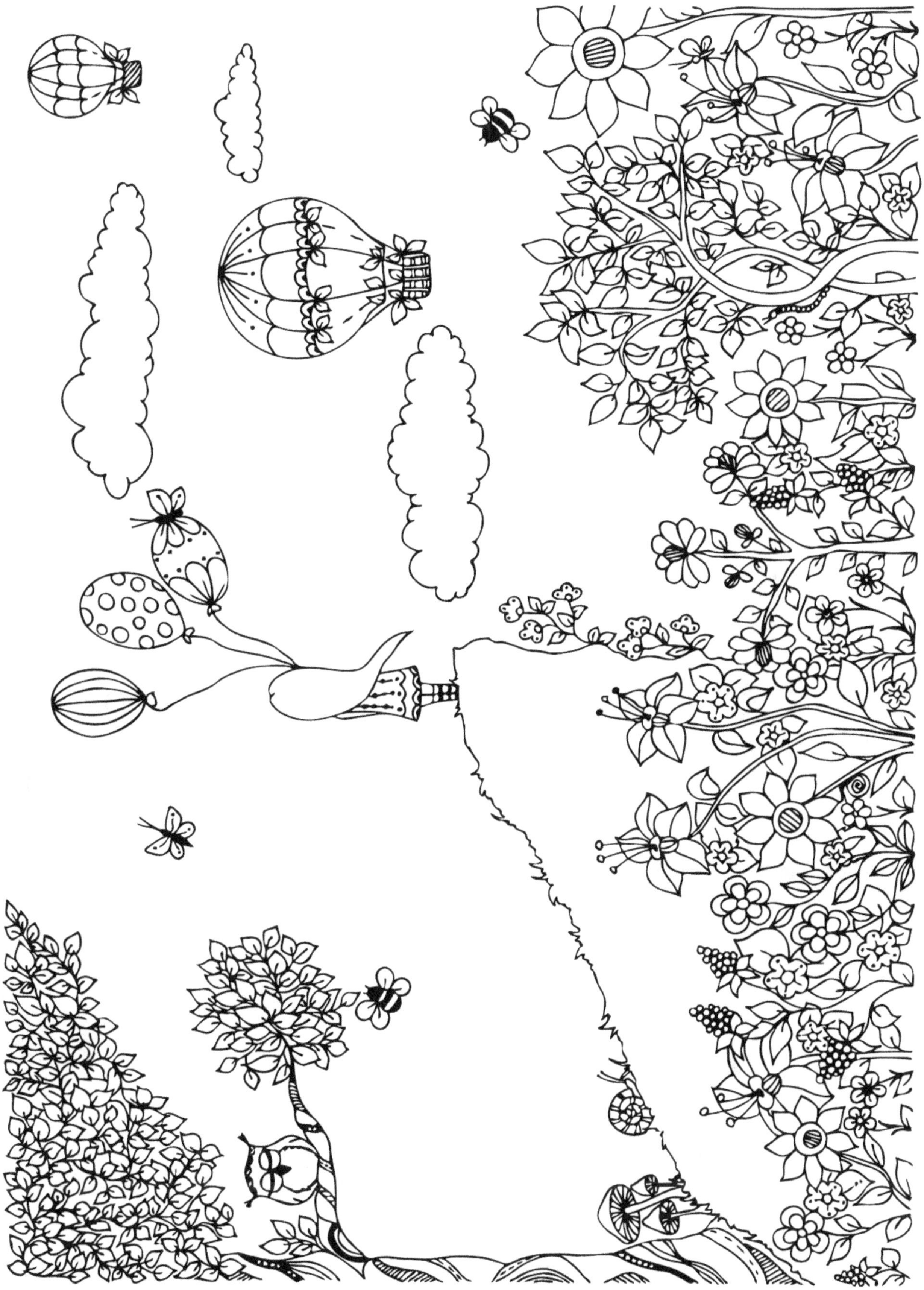

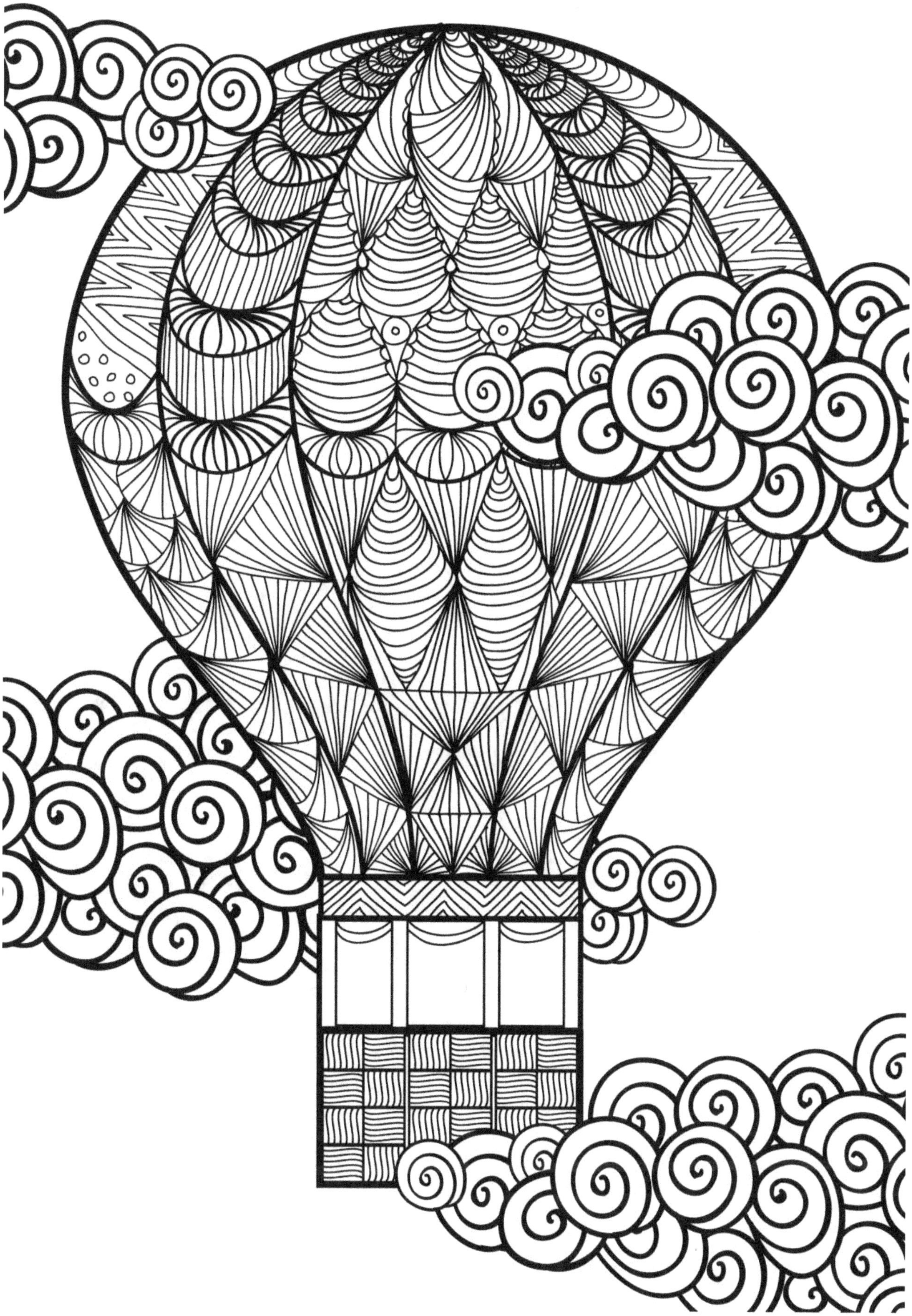

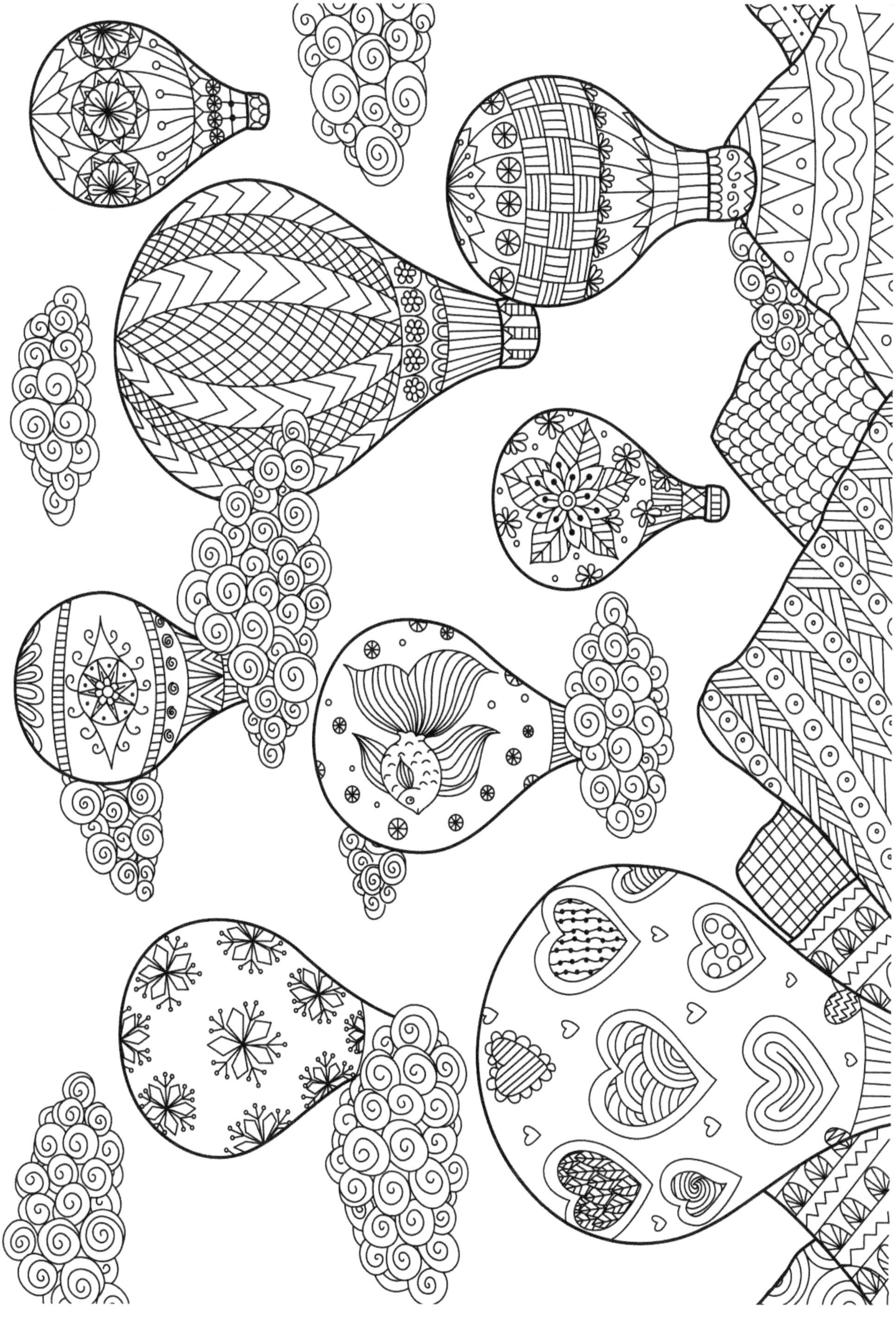

TRAVEL

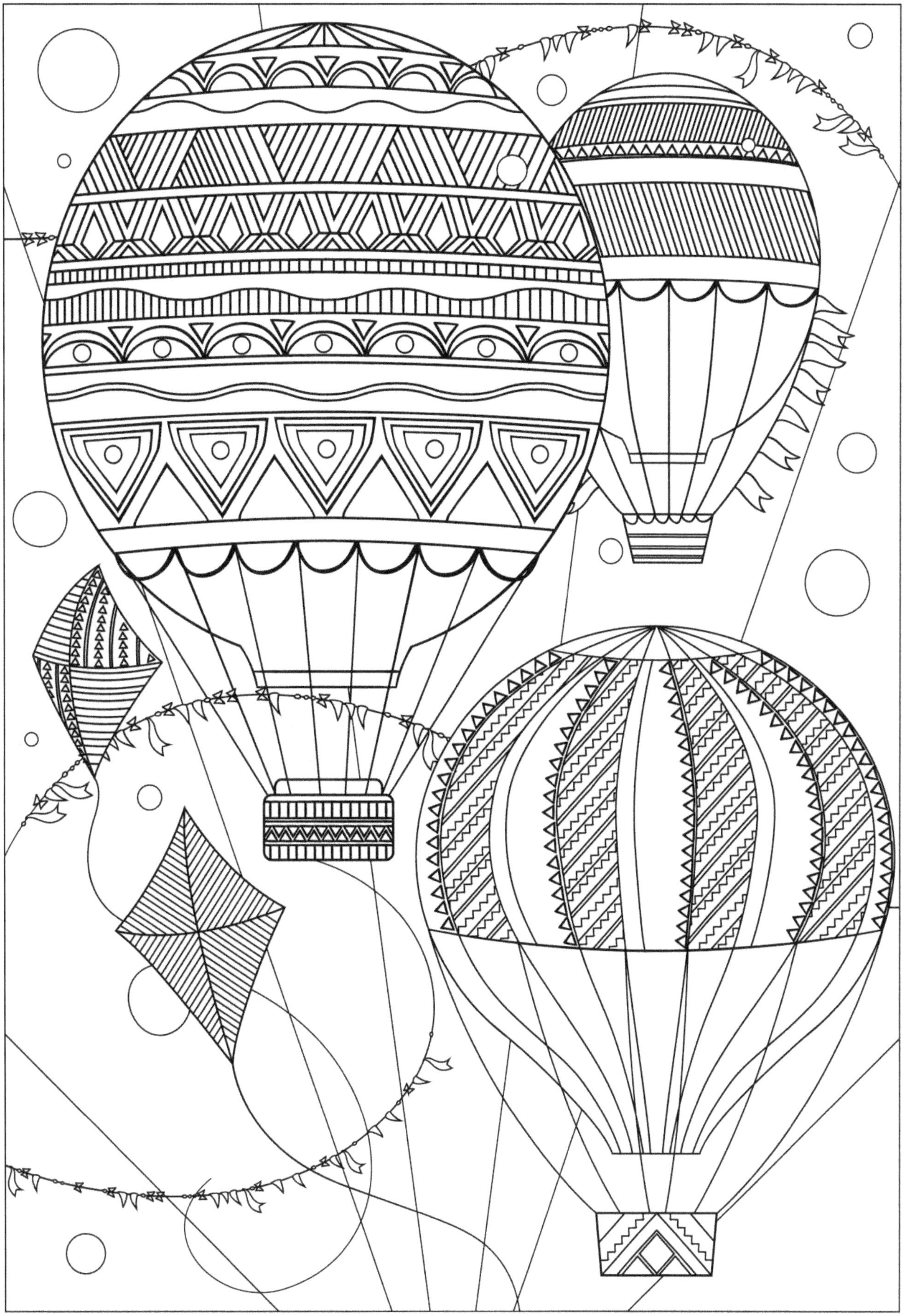

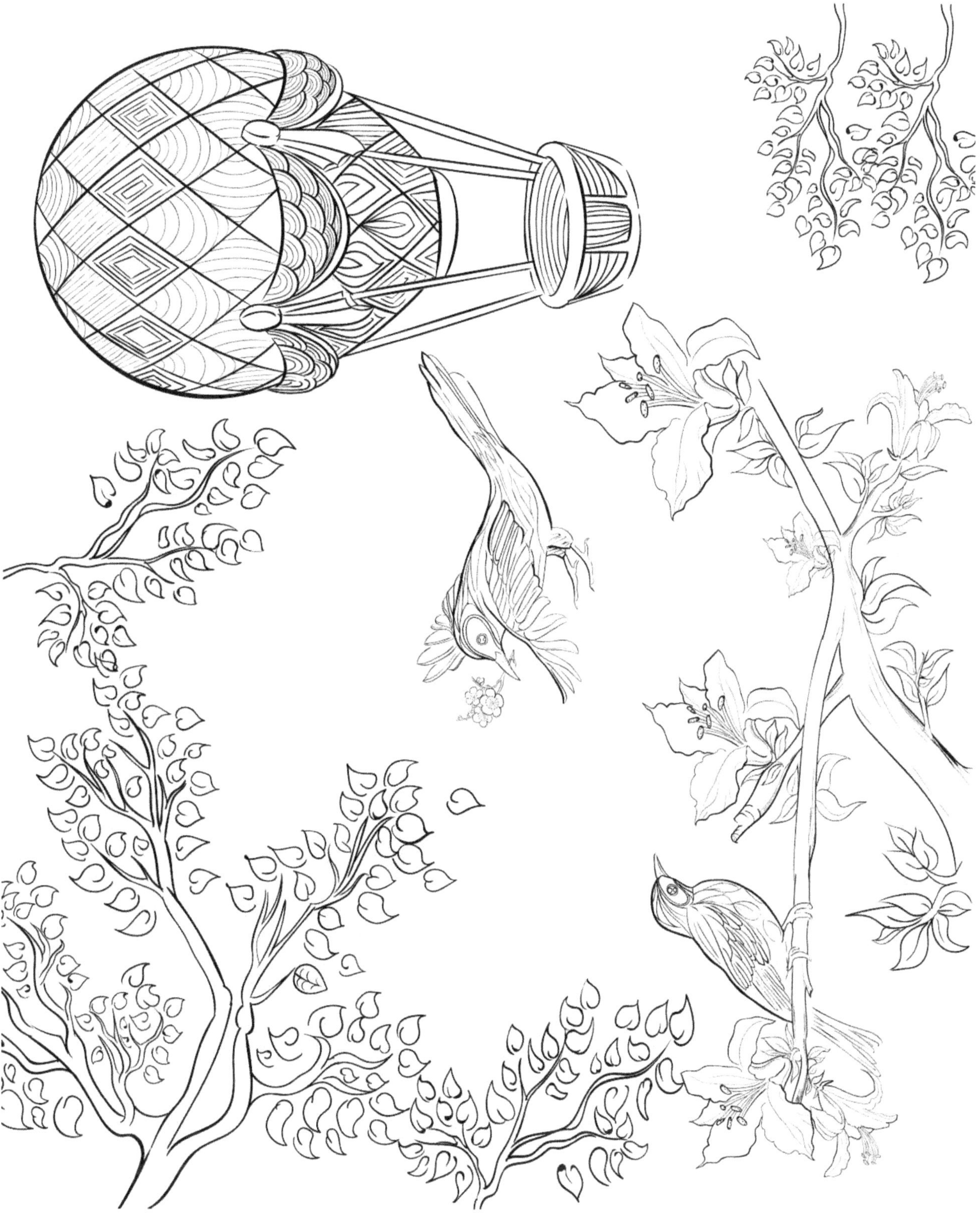

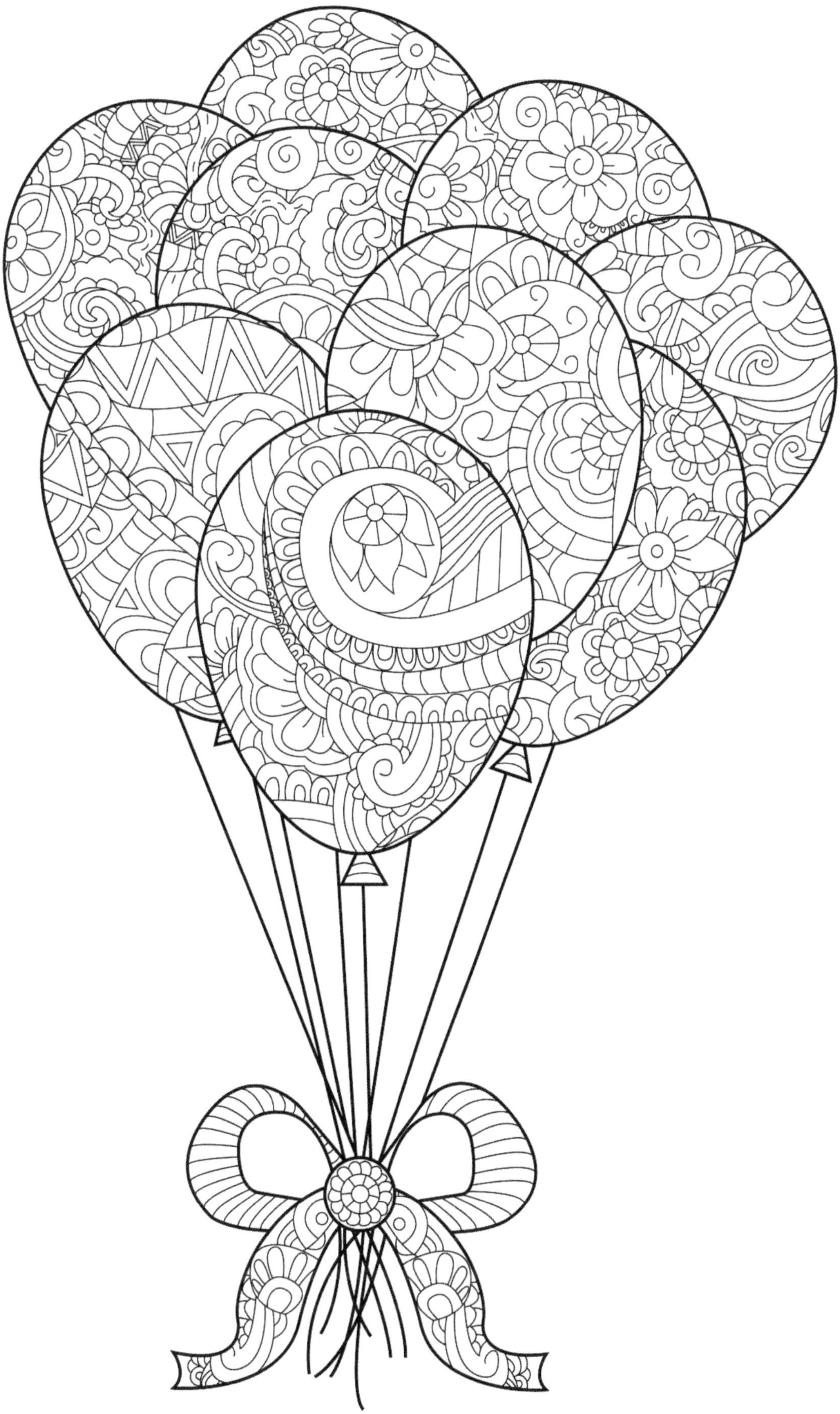

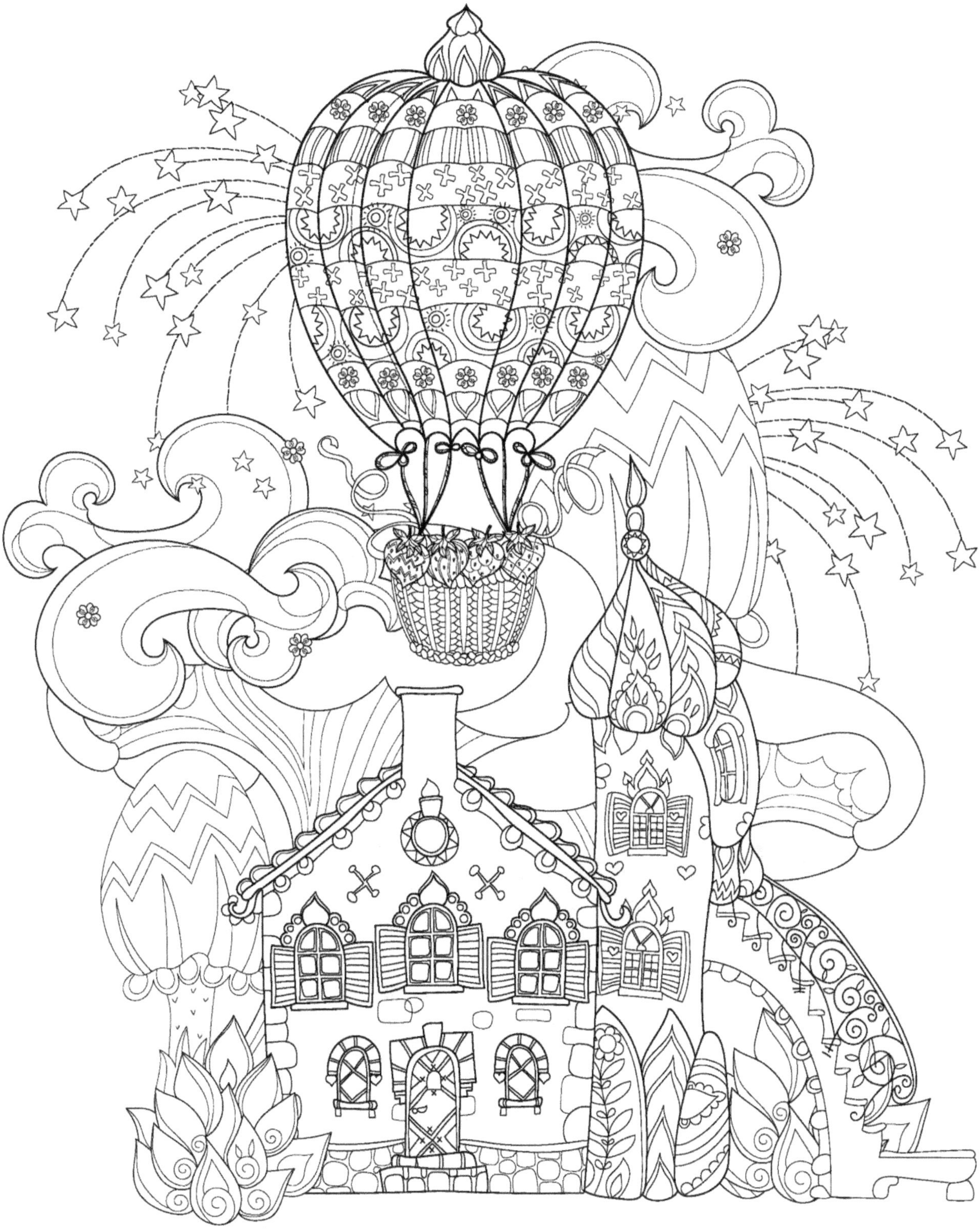

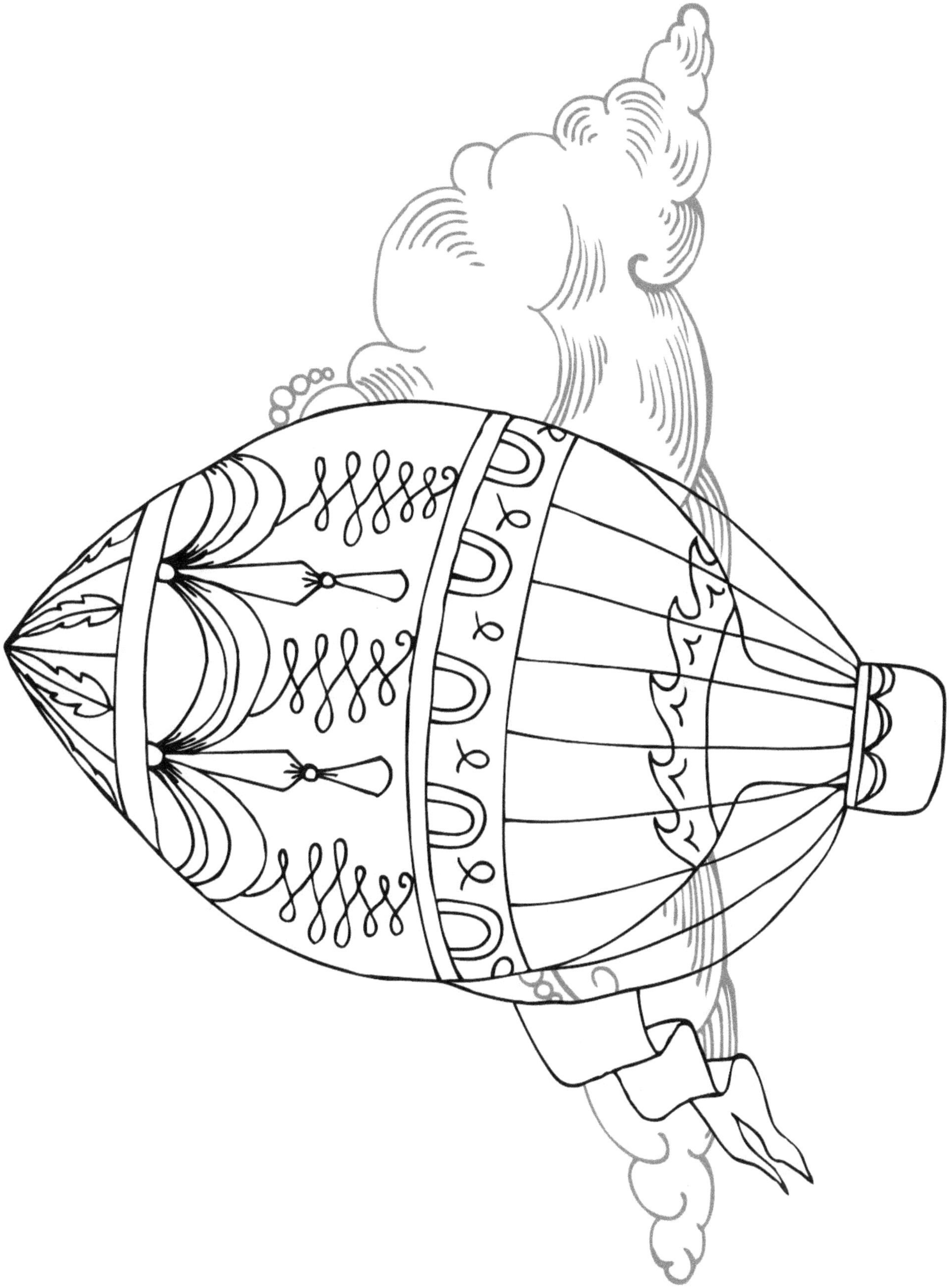

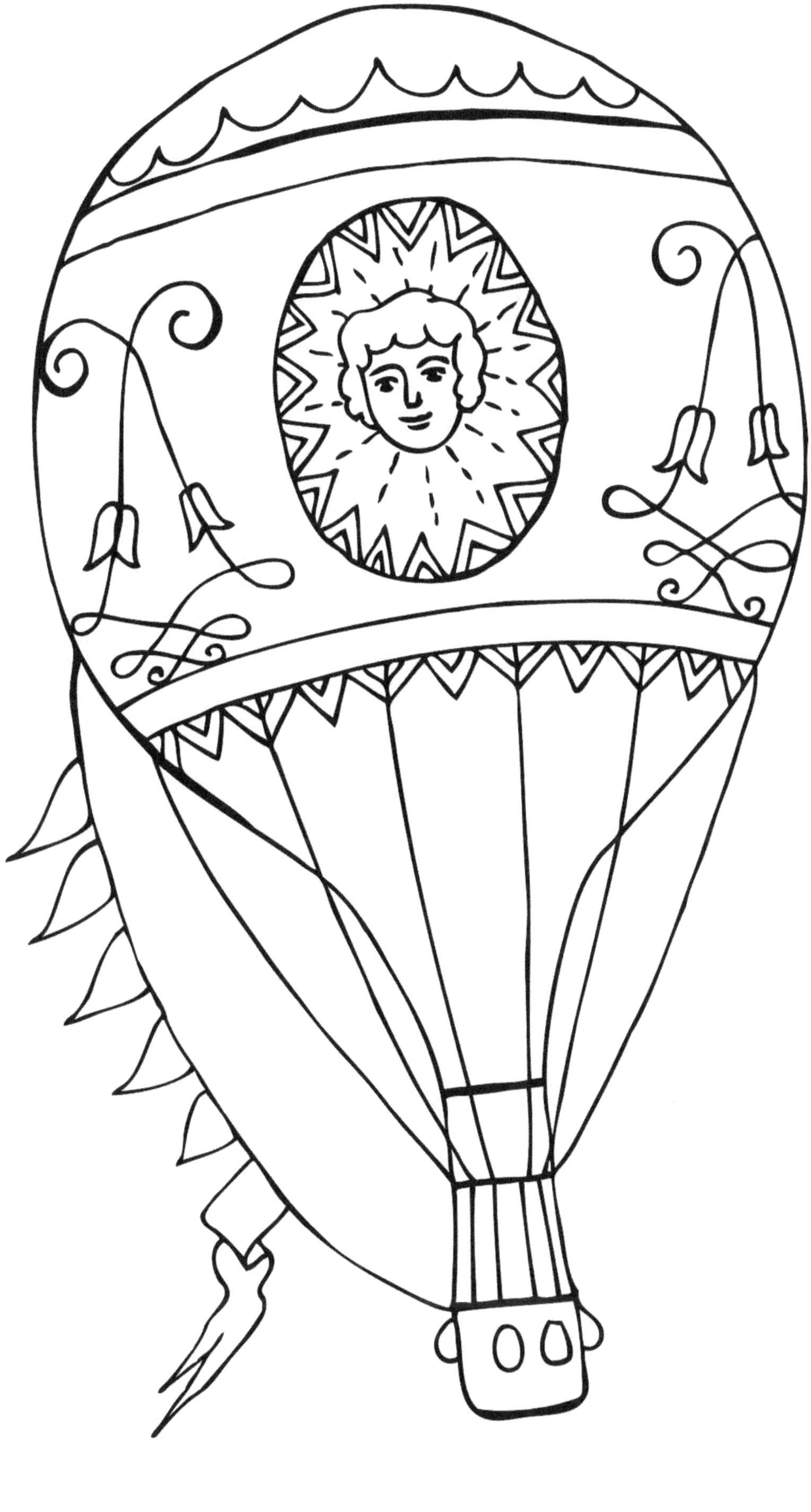

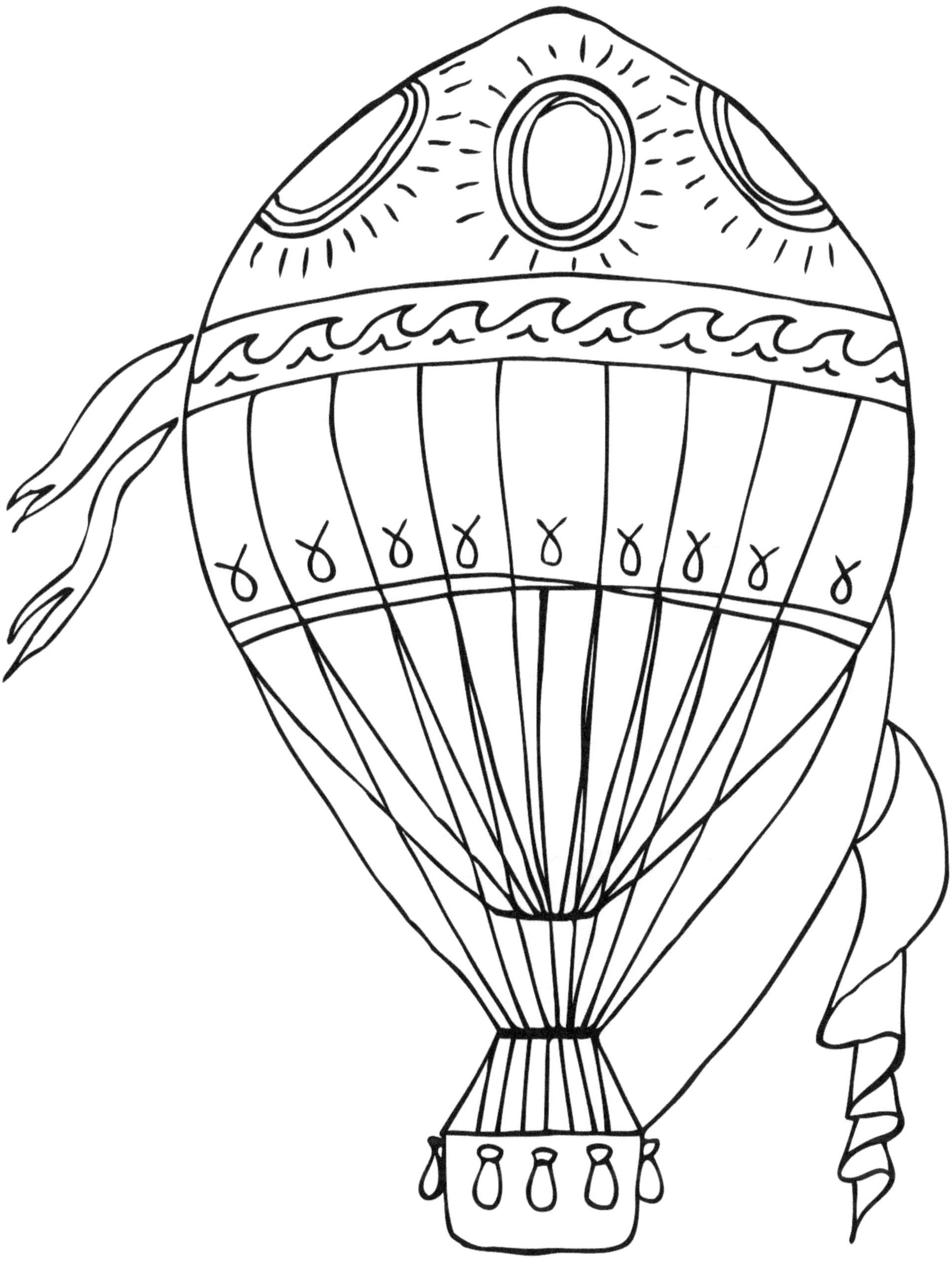

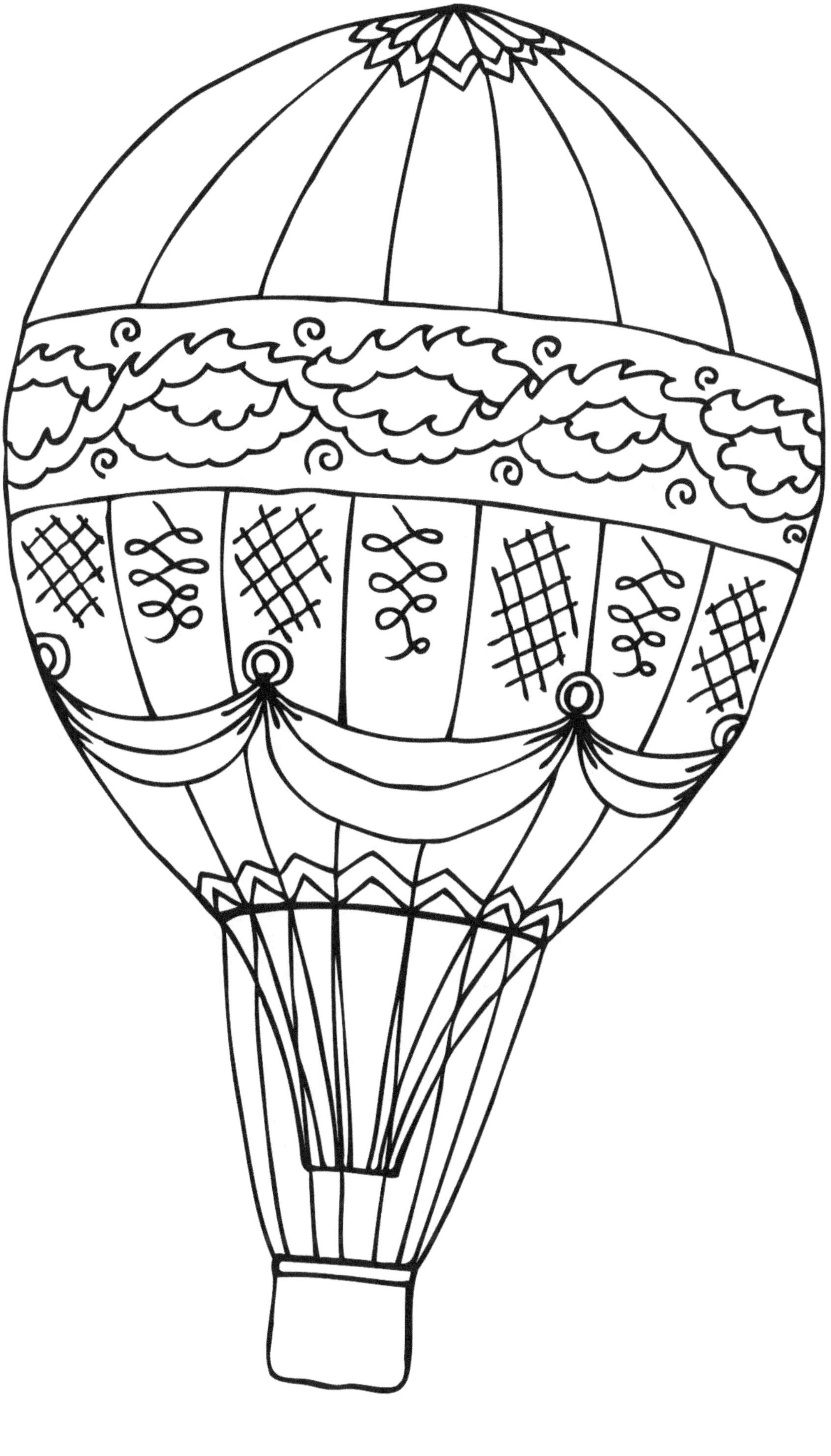

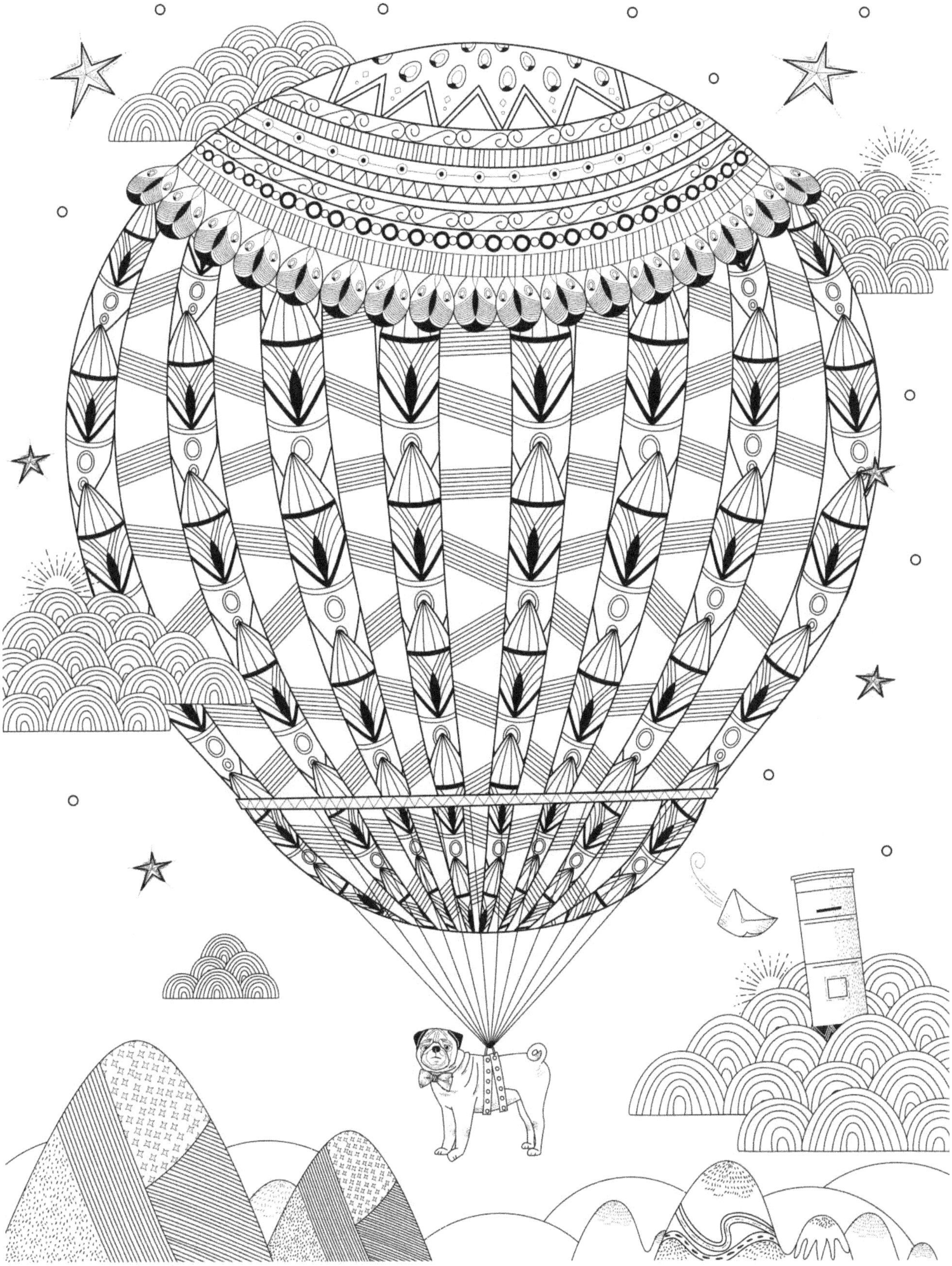

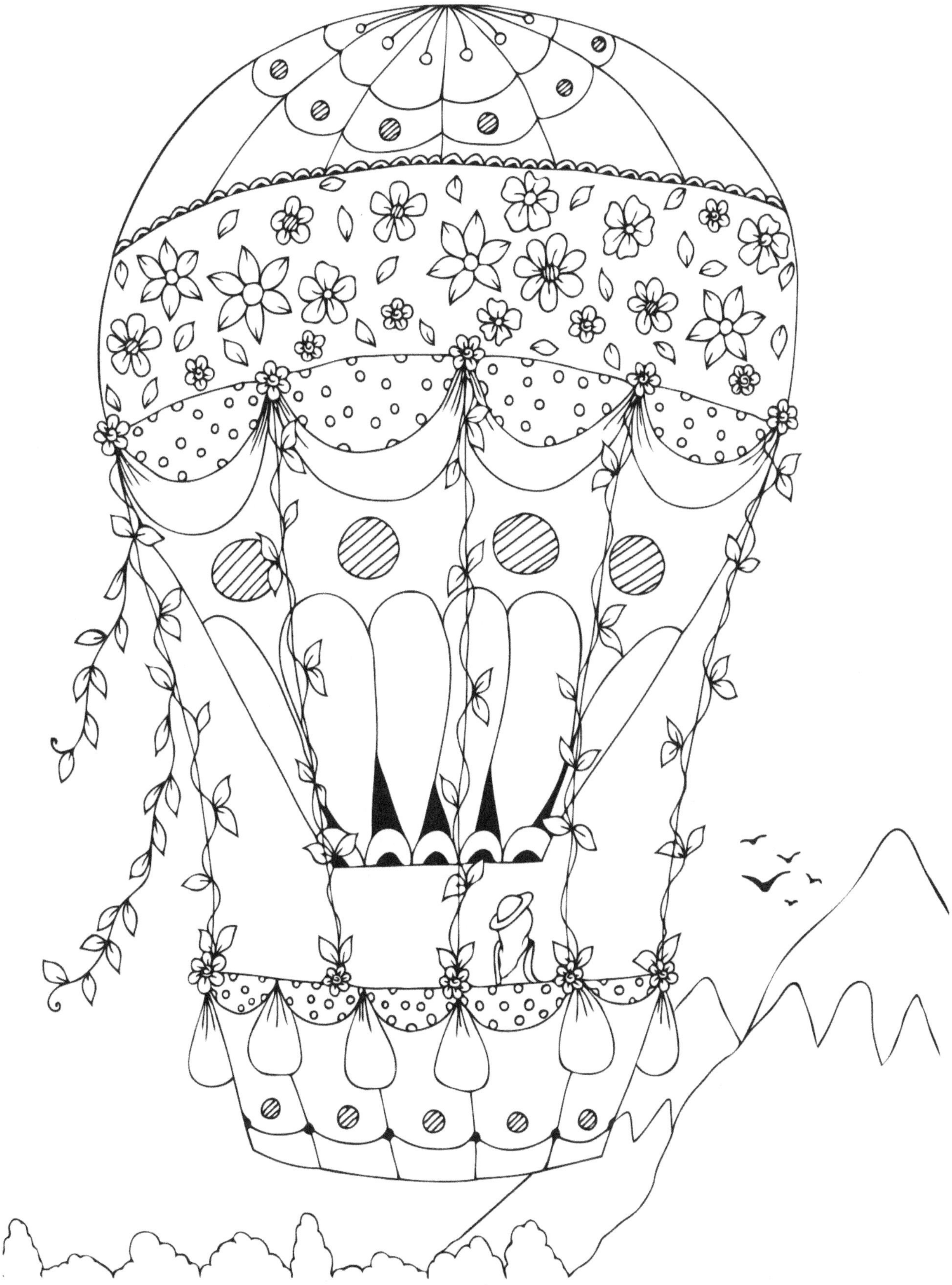

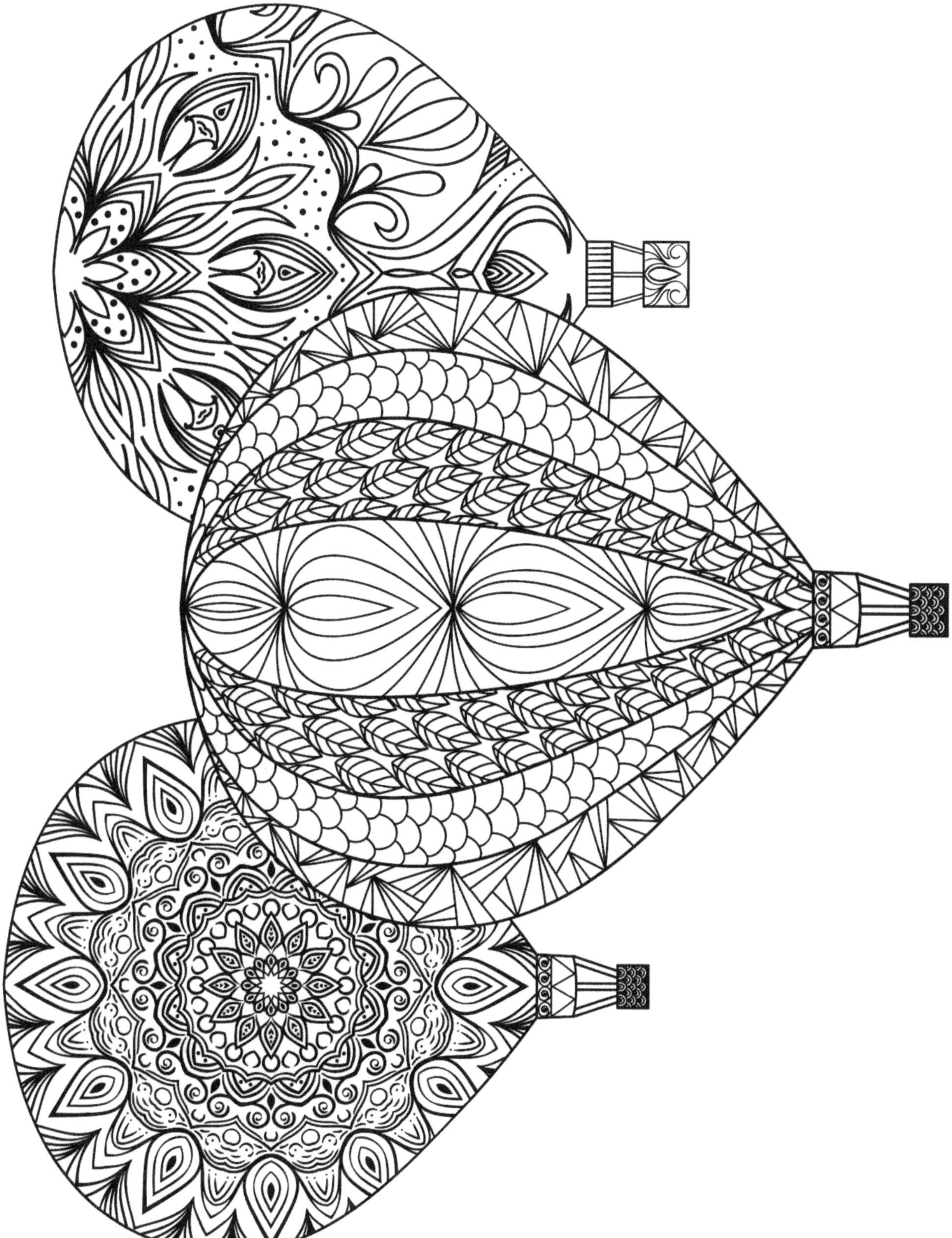

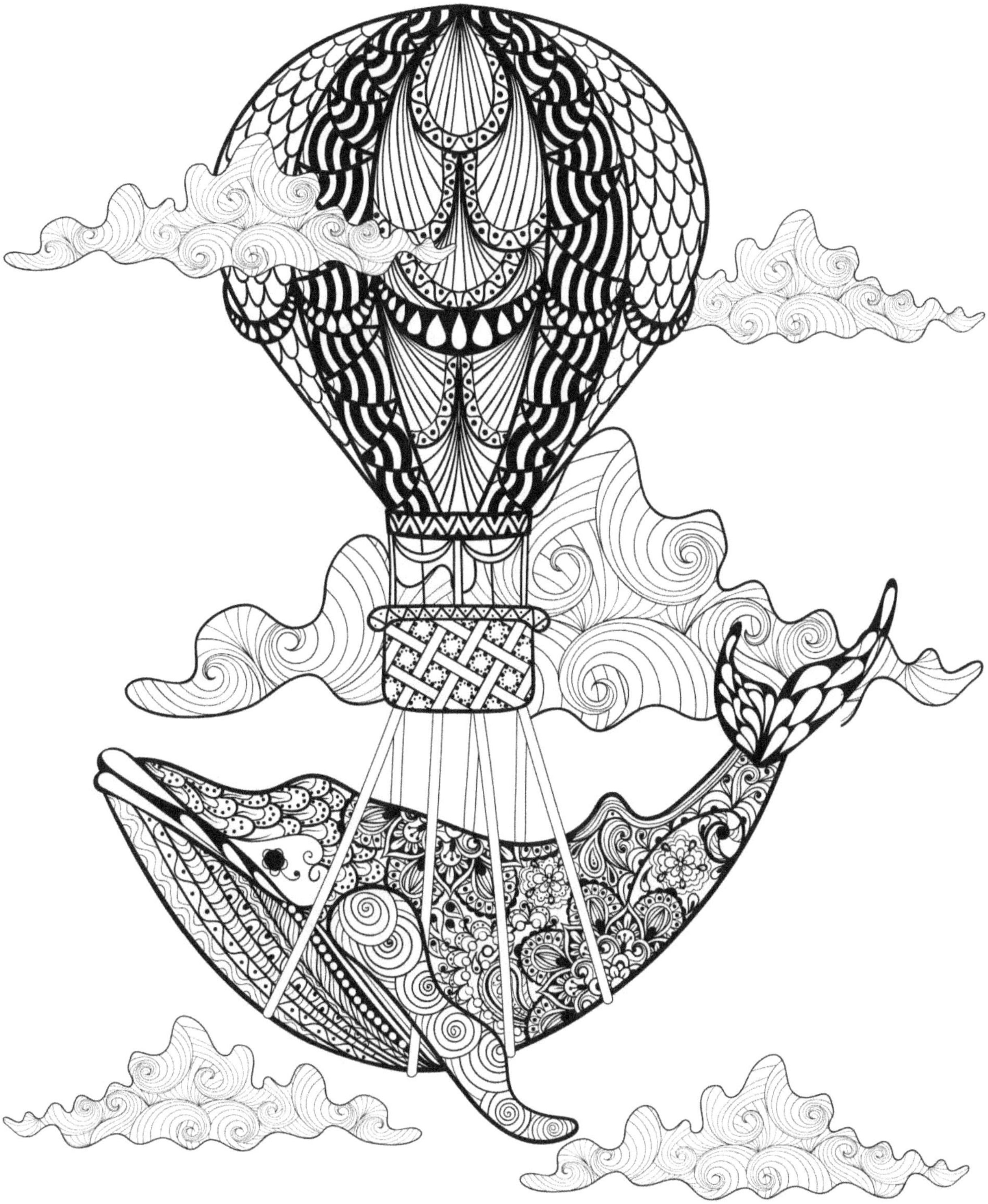

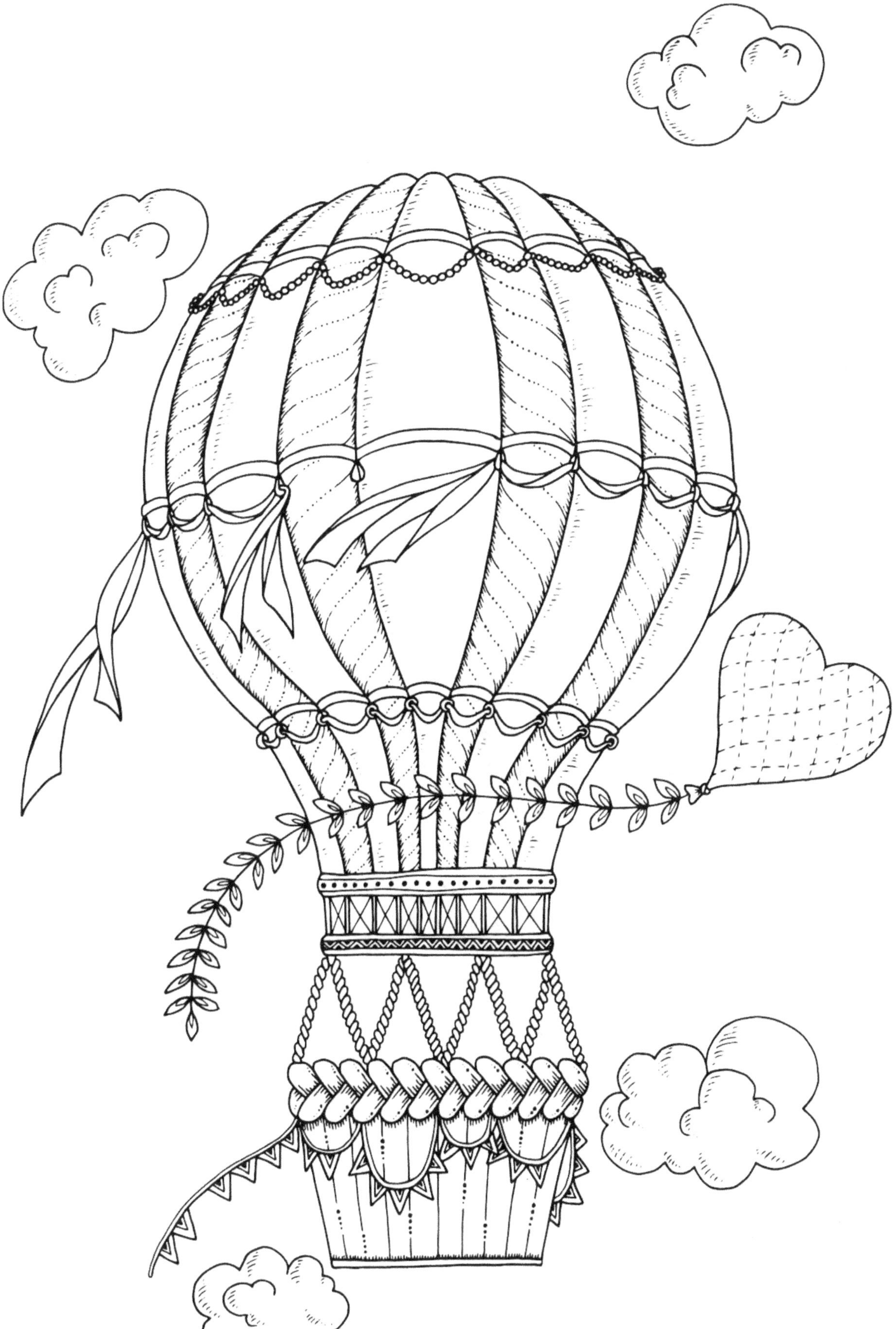

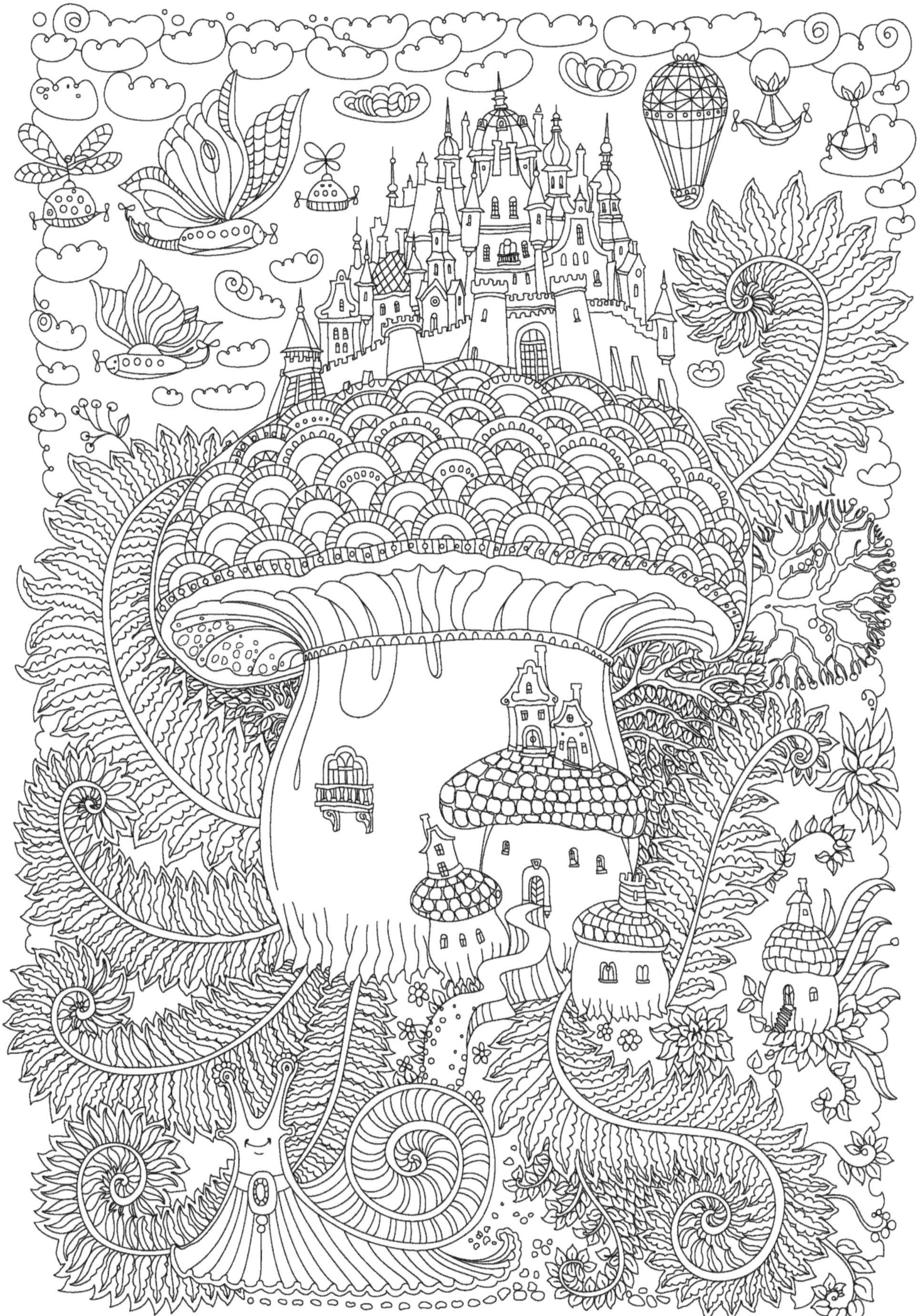

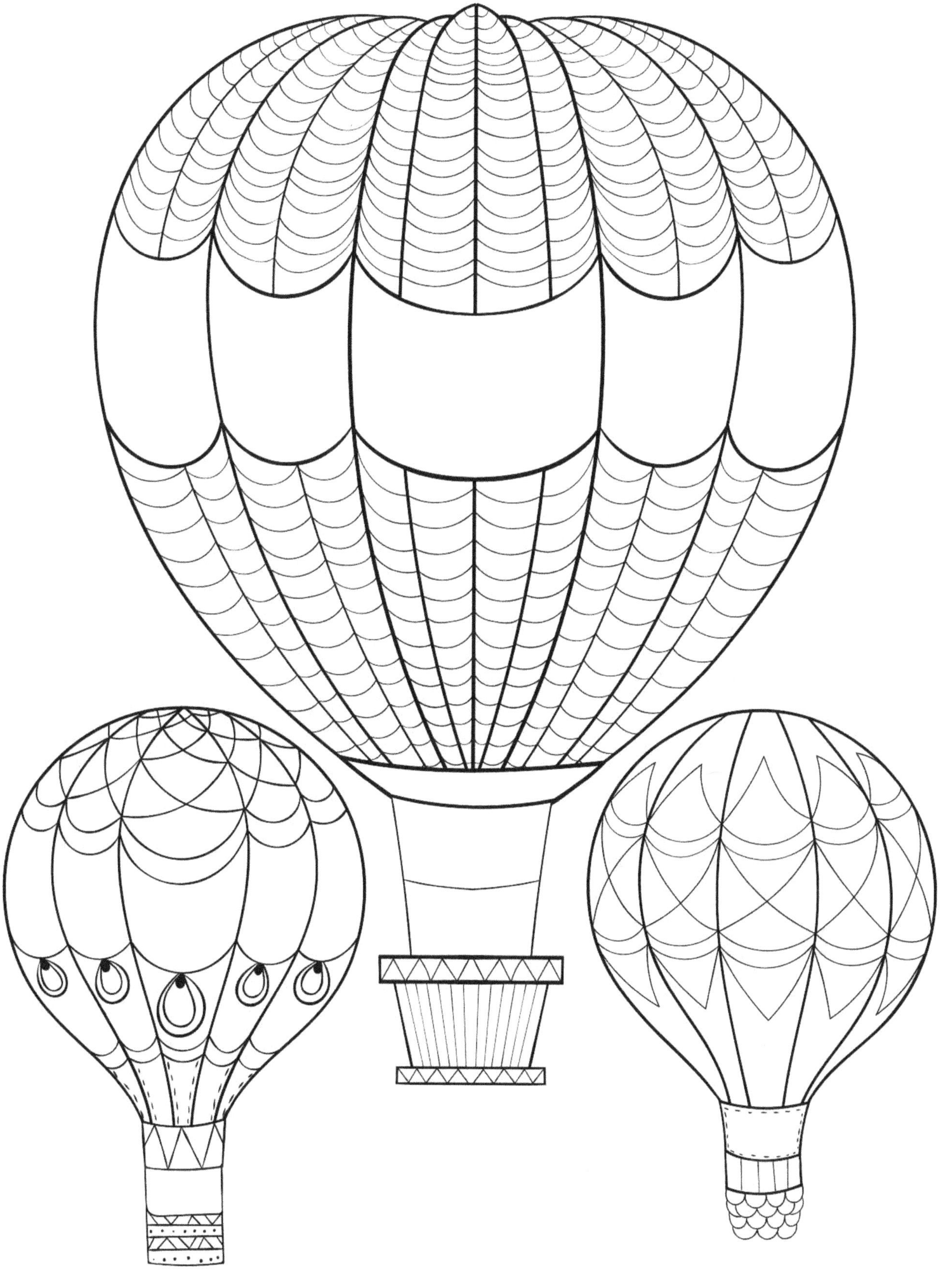

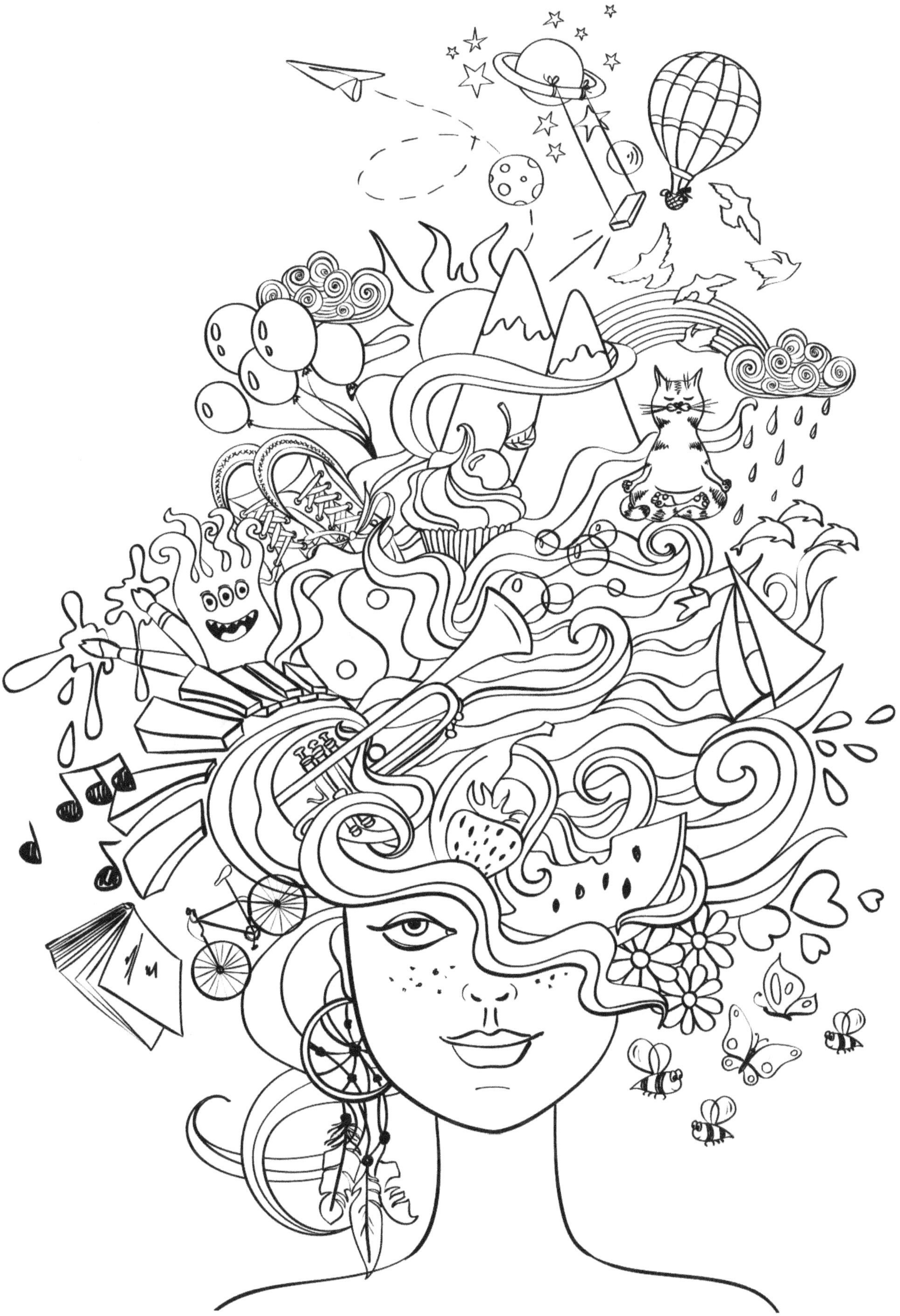

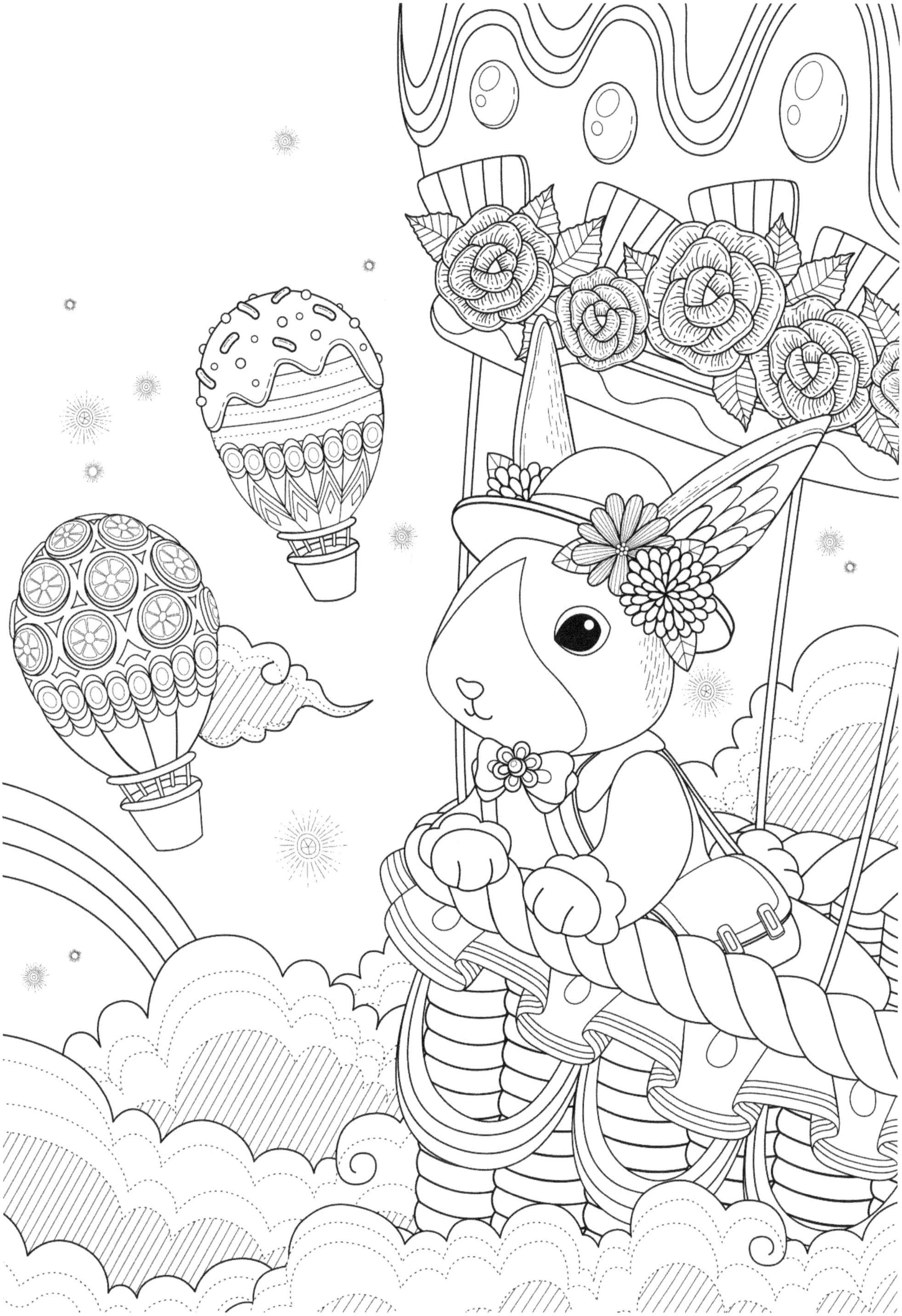

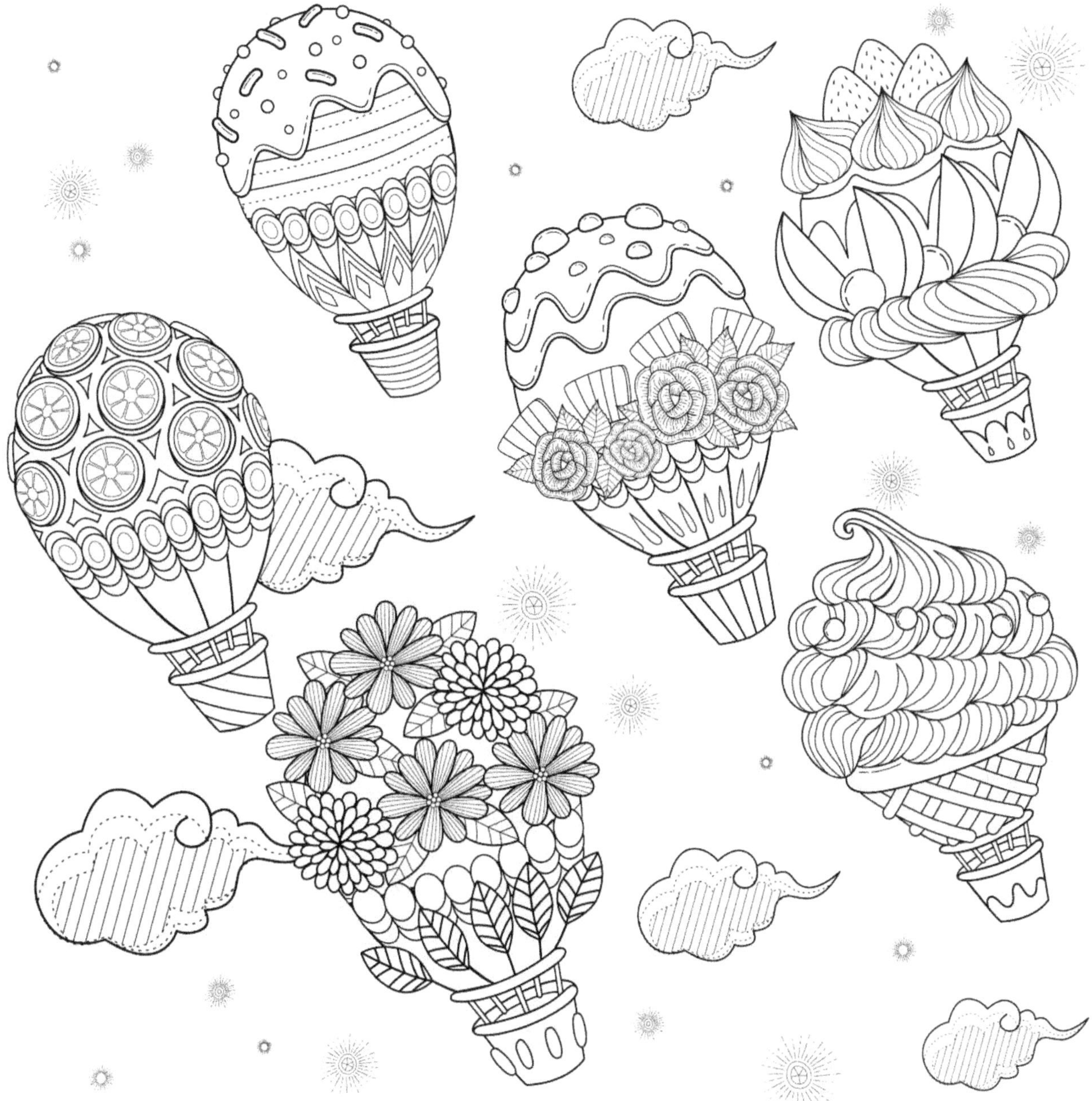

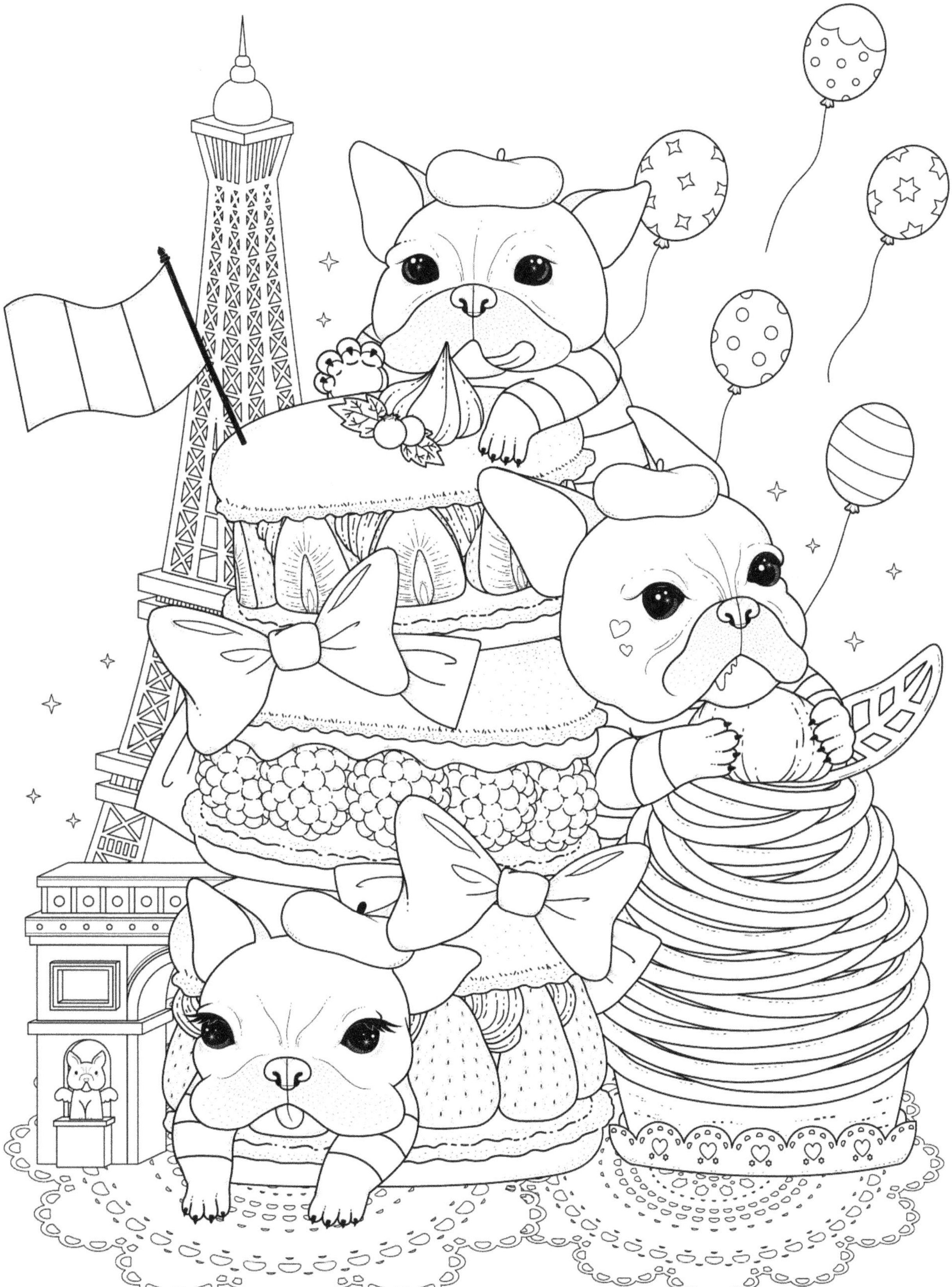

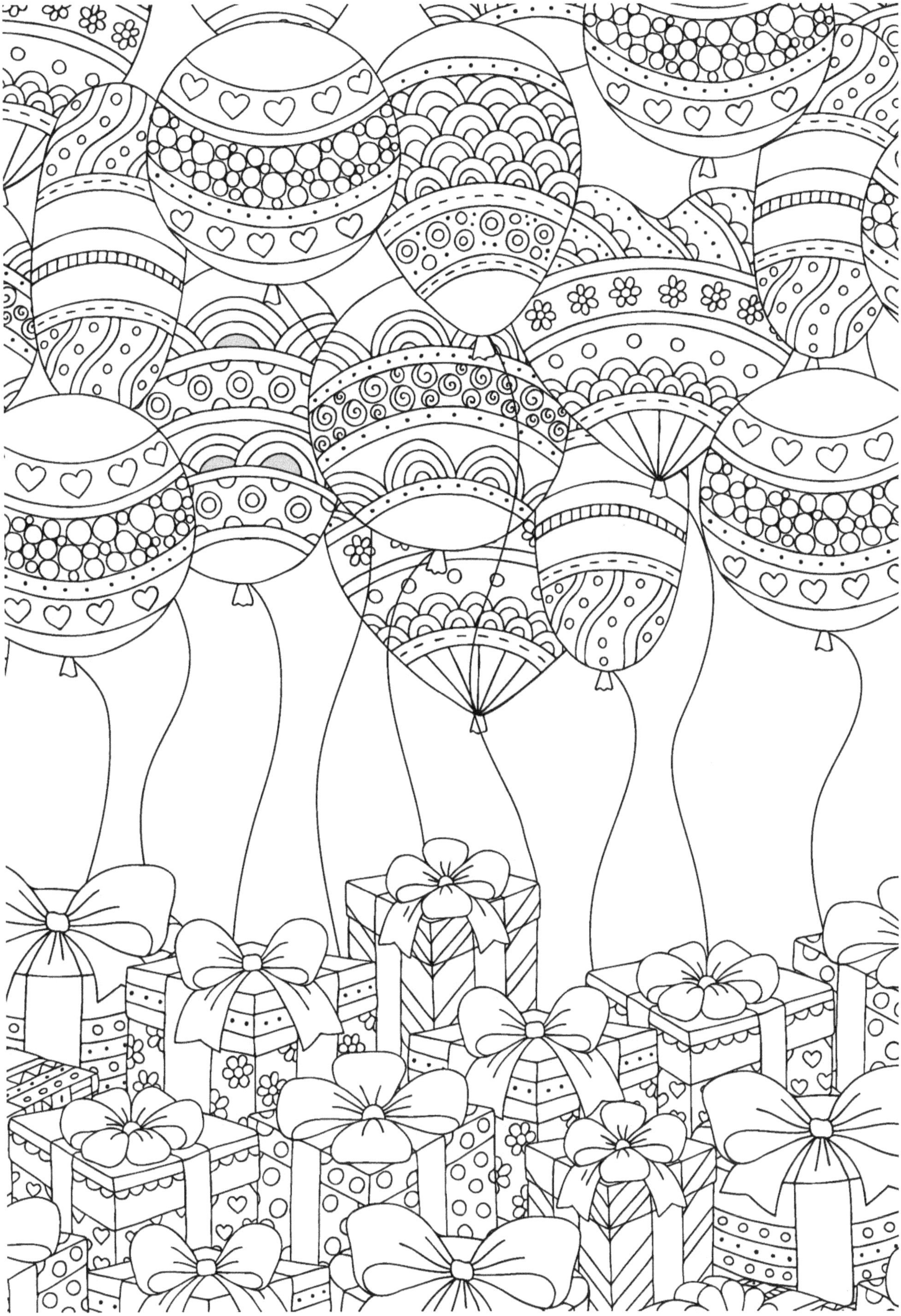

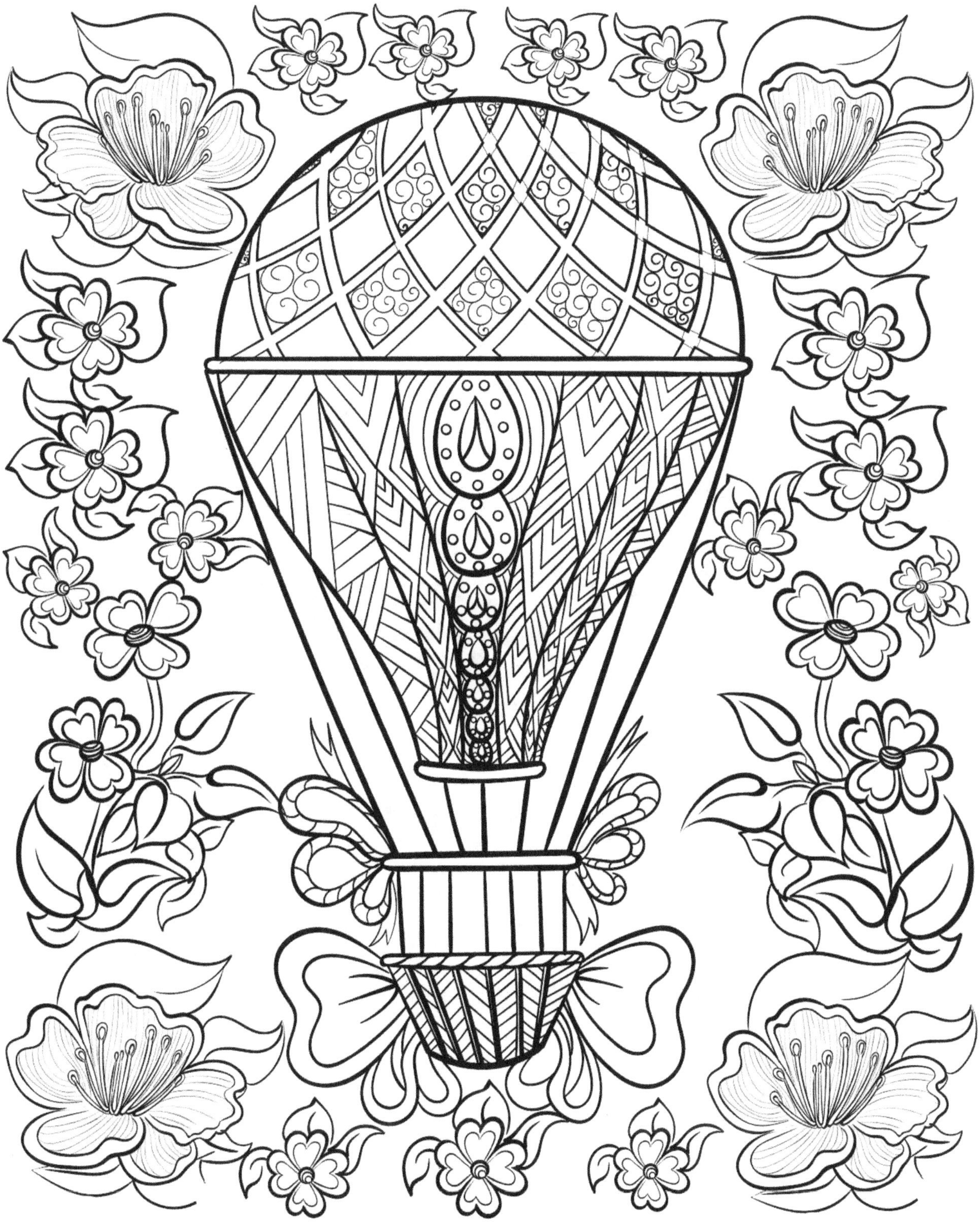

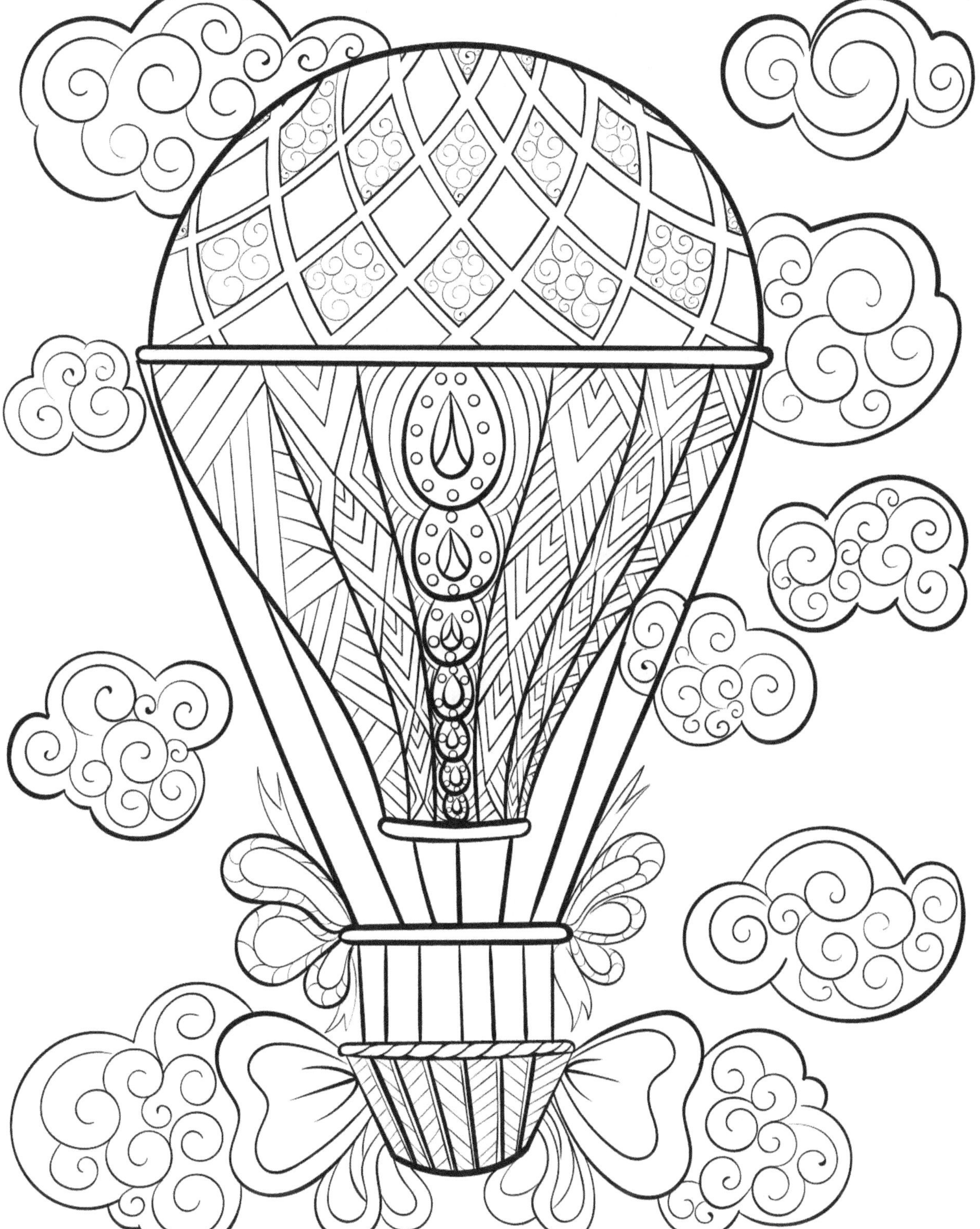

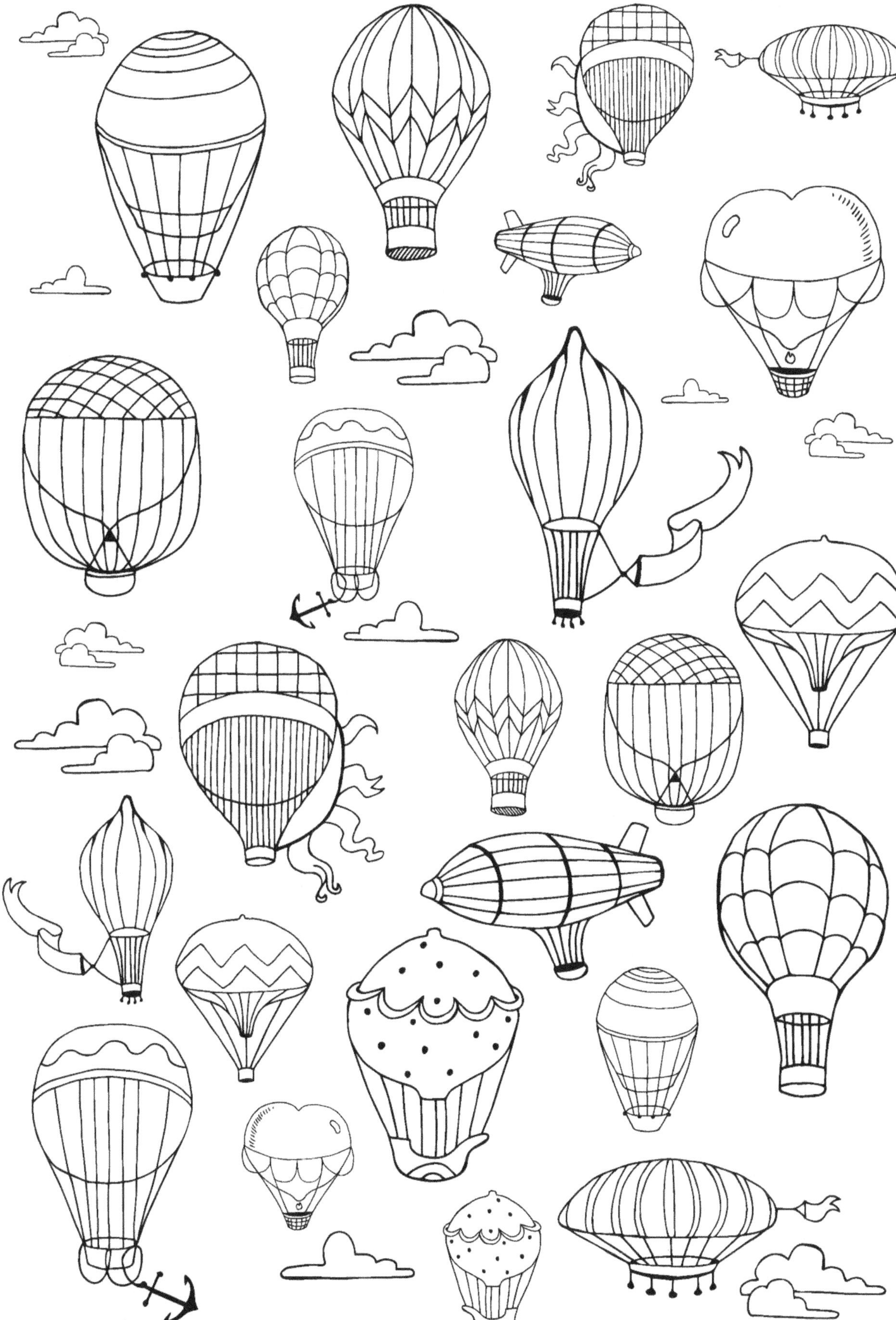

www.ingramcontent.com/pod-product-compliance
Lightning Source LLC
Chambersburg PA
CBHW081851170526
45167CB00007B/2972
* 9 7 8 1 5 4 3 0 3 0 6 2 4 *